The Pastor's Secrets
Volume 1

Debra B. Spencer

Disclaimer

Scripture taken from the

HOLY BIBLE, NEW INTERNATIONAL VERSION,

Copyright © 1973, 1978, 1984 International Society

Used by permission of Zondervan Bible Publishers

THE PASTOR'S SECRETS

VOLUME ONE

MESSAGE FROM THE GRAVE

SAY IT AIN'T SO

Dedication

Dedicated to my Grandparents

Rev. Alec & Nannie Brewer

Deacon Jerry & Deaconess Nellie Mingo

and Charles Y. Alston

I know that you are smiling in heaven.

&

John H. Spencer, III,

Because you remind us daily that

Love Never Dies.

Acknowledgements

Thank you to my wonderful husband, Rev. Dr. John H. Spencer, Jr. for your patience, love and support. Thank you to my son, Minister William "BJ" Simmons, III, for your encouragement and inspiration and to my daughter-in-law Qianna for filling my life with joy. Thank you to my beloved grandchildren, Aniya, Bill and John - John, always remember that Mama Debra loves you. Thank you to my parents, John & Elfrieta Brewer, without whom this book would not have been possible and to my sisters Tami & Kim for reading and re-reading and re-reading my stories and to my brothers, Donnie & Michael for believing in me. Thank you to my "Baby Girl" Tramia, Kachiri, Jarrid and Todd for helping me find OZ. Thank you to my always supportive mother-in-law, Mrs. Lillian Spencer and sister-friend Helen Coleman. Thank you to my "brother & sister in Christ," Rev. Gregory & Barbara Jackson & the Mount Olive Baptist Church Family of Hackensack, NJ for your prayers and continued support. A very special thank you to Keisha McLean and Minister Sanetta Ponton for all of your help with the book. Even as a writer, I have no words to truly express how much I appreciate and love my First Baptist Church, Englewood, NJ Family, so I simply say thank you for everything.

Last but not least I thank God for the blessing of

knowing that my salvation is secure. My desire is to

glorify You and to minister to Your people!

Table of Contents

Message From The Grave

Prelude: Ready or Not

As he drove from his home to the church, Rev. Branford could see the sun beginning to make its appearance from behind the blue-black haze of the night sky. He drove slowly along the empty streets imagining God spitting the fiery sphere from his mouth. He envisioned God opening his mouth wider, and wider pushing the flaming star out past his lips until all of the remnants of the night entirely disappeared signaling the start of a new day. Although the morning skies had been blue and bright all week, Rev. Branford could not have imagined the storm that awaited him at Hope & Grace Christian Center the day before. Branford had served as pastor of Hope and Grace for nine months. But yesterday was the first time he had questioned whether or not he was ready for the responsibility of being their spiritual leader. None of his ministerial training or even his life experiences had truly prepared him for the test he faced. It was a trial-by-fire day if ever there were one.

Chapter 1: Penny's Trap

Pulling into the driveway, Rev. Branford noted to himself that the church parking lot was already full. "Thank God for the reserved parking space for the pastor or I might not have a place to park my car," he thought as he grinned mischievously to himself. "Now, wouldn't that be a crying shame, I'd just have to go back home and get in my nice, warm bed," he thought as he turned into his parking space.

Springing from the car, he jogged briskly the few paces from his parking space to the church building eager to begin his day. "The sooner the day begins the sooner I can get back home," the pastor thought. He had missed dinner with his family the night before because his meeting with a member, Kitera Davidson, had taken longer than he had anticipated. "I can't be late tonight," he reminded himself. He had promised his daughter Penny that he would be home for dinner in time to help her with her self-imposed homework assignment tonight for sure. The night before when he got home, Penny was already in bed. She was asleep or pretending to be at least when he tried unsuccessfully to slip quietly into her room to give her a good night kiss. Going into her room, he was unaware of the funny and devilish plan she had made to trap him. 'Penny is always good for a laugh," he thought.

Knowing that her Dad always came into her room, to give her a good night kiss, no matter what time he got home, she sprawled all of her squeaky toys over the floor hoping that he would step on one before he could turn on the light. Of course, he had done just what she had imagined he would do. He'd stepped on a loud squeaky toy before he could get to the light switch and see all of the dollies and other playthings laying atop the dusty rose colored carpet.

Branford was not sure which noise woke her - the squeaking toy or his yelp from being shocked when his barefoot landed on her slimy feeling rubber frog.

But Penny sat straight up in her bed immediately and began badgering him about where he had been and why he was so late.

"Daddy, you know I need your help. Abigail and Jai already know how to make cursive letters. I want to know, too. Do you really want me to be the only kid in this house who only knows how to print, Daddy? Do you, Daddy? Penny had asked without taking a breath or waiting for an answer. I want to write my name pretty like they do, Daddy. You said you would show me again tonight how to write my name," she pouted.

Guilty as charged, he had acknowledged to her. He knew no excuse would be good enough for Penny, so he simply said, "I'll be home in time to help you with your homework tomorrow, okay?"

"Promise?" she said.

"Yes, I promise. Now get up and help me pick up this stuff before your mother comes in here in the morning and trips over something and hurts herself."

"That would be big trouble right?" Penny asked although she already knew the answer.

"Yes, big trouble for both of us," he chuckled.

"But I did catch you, didn't I Daddy," she said as they both reached for the last of the toys she had scattered on the floor. "I knew you would come in here tonight to give me a kiss. It was a good trap wasn't it?"

"You mean you left all of this stuff on the floor on purpose?"

"Yes, otherwise I would have stayed sleep when you came in, and I would have missed getting to remind you that I need you to help me with the cursive writing."

"I see," he said.

"It was a good trap, right? Just like the one you and I made for the Tooth Fairy, remember Daddy?"

"Yes, I remember."

"But we didn't catch the Tooth Fairy, she must have flown over everything, but I caught you, Daddy. I am glad that you can't fly."

"Really, you wouldn't want to see me flying around your room dressed like the Tooth Fairy in a leotard and little blue tutu?"

"No, Daddy that would be too silly. But this was a good trap, huh, Daddy wasn't it."

"Yes, it was a good trap, Penny he said, remembering their recent Tooth Fairy caper. But don't ever do it again. Okay? I could have fallen and hurt myself, baby girl." Penny didn't answer she just turned and smiled her best, "but I'm the baby" smile at him.

"I mean it Penny," he said in a stern voice, not sure if he was getting through to her. Penny kept smiling but did not say a word.

"Back to bed now, you," Branford said as he lifted his wiggling daughter up and gently tossed her on the bed. Penny scrambled under the covers.

"Love you, Daddy," she said as he tucked the pink scalloped blanket up under her chin and kissed her forehead.

"Love you too, Penny. Sleep tight."

"Don't let the bed bugs bite," she finished the line for him. He winked at her and turned off the light. Heading down the hall he made sure he checked the floor before he stepped into his son, Jai's room.

Penny, short for Penelope was six years old and the youngest of his three children. She was feisty with a bubbly personality and a laugh that was contagious. Most of all she had his heart twisted around her little finger. She was a Daddy's girl, and he was proud to be her Dad. Abigail, the oldest was studious, and unlike her sister Penny she was fiercely independent, always eager to do everything on her own. Lately, Abigail seemed to be transforming before his eyes from his little tomboy in braids and sneakers into a charming young girl with a budding interest in the boys she once called knuckleheads and played basketball against and won. Jai, his son had a quick wit that Branford loved. He was affable, good-natured, and much easier to get along with than either of his girls.

Joshua hated disappointing the kids by not being home for dinner as often as he should and was always feeling guilty about not being able to give them all of the attention they craved, especially Penny.

Joshua's thoughts about the previous night began to wane as he put his key in the lock, and pulled on the silver doorknob of the church. But the smile on his face remained, as the sight of Penny's trap, and his realization that his wife, Megan surely had her hands full with their kids, crystalized in his mind. Giving Megan a break by occupying the kids for a while would make them happy and surely would not hurt his love life either. "Yes, got to get home early tonight," he thought.

Rev. Branford pounced up the stairs to the church office two at a time while thinking to himself, "this is a great way to start off a Wednesday. Yes, this is a great way to start off a Wednesday," he repeated.

Making encouraging affirmations to himself was his way of psyching himself up for the members, he and some of his older congregants jokingly called the Wake the Dead group. "Full speed ahead," he thought.

Chapter 2: Hope and Grace Christian Center

Energetic and all prayed up seemed the best way to describe those gathered for the Wake the Dead Wednesday's 6:00AM Prayer Service.

Thinking of how the people who attended this service were once nick-named the Faithful Few Crew because there had only been about a dozen or so members who were willing to come out for a 6:00AM service, he smiled to himself. Now he could take pleasure in the fact that now there were almost as many folk at the Wednesday morning 6:00AM service as there were at the Sunday morning 11:00AM service. However, the service had undoubtedly been taken over by a younger, more enthusiastic, and animated crowd. In fact, unless they had on hearing aids that could be turned down, most of the older members could not tolerate the loud music, singing, drums and tambourines. In fact, the service got its name, *Wake the Dead Wednesday*, when one angry member said some people praying were loud enough to wake the dead and refused to attend any more services even after he reminded her there were many verses in the Bible that encouraged people to shout with joy and sing with loud voices to the Lord. "Come on," he had said, "You know Psalm 100 by heart. We say it all of the time, 'Make joyful noises unto the Lord.'" Interrupting him before he could finish, she pointed her finger at him and said, "Pastor, there ain't that much joy in the world. They just fools, Pastor, just fools."

"Sorry that you feel that way," he remembered saying.

She said, "Me, too," and stomped away.

He was not sure if she meant that she was sorry that he felt the way he did or that she felt the way she did.

It did not matter however because either way so far she had been true to her word. She did not come back.

Even though, some of his members didn't like it, he had actually grown to love the Wednesday morning worshipers. The service was filled with adult working folk - bus drivers, teachers, Post Office workers, nurses and laborers. These were people who by Wednesday had had their fill of superior acting supervisors, bumbling bosses and criticizing customers and clients. They let go of their frustrations as they sang, shouted and prayed for the ability to hold on to that job or marriage or enough money to put food on the table. They began each service with the Call to Worship, from Psalm 47:1-2

Clap your hands, all you nations;
    shout to God with cries of joy.
For the LORD Most High is awesome,
    the great King over all the earth.

And they took the words seriously. United, they sang God's praises, shouted for joy, played instruments loudly, wept profusely then left the sanctuary and sanctity of the church to fight seemingly single-handedly unholy and unwholesome battles in the world.

It was 5:45AM and he could already hear someone shouting "Thank you, Jesus." He did not know if they found a job or lost one and were thanking God for the better one, they believed was coming. Either way, their shouts were true to form, loud enough to *Wake the Dead.*

Greeted at the door, Pastor Branford said, "Morning, Deacon Felder. Thank you for opening up this morning. I see people are already fired up."

"Yes, Pastor. Some are glad to be here, and some are just glad to be out of the cold," the Deacon responded.

"I know that's the truth. I will be out shortly." Pastor Branford said as he headed to his office.

"That's fine; Annabel already made coffee and tea, would you like a cup before you go in."

"Sure, tea with honey and lemon. Is she baking, too?"

"Of course, I'll bring you back whatever is ready."

"If it is her airy-flairy yeast rolls bring me two."

"I guess that name is official now for Annabel's rolls," Deacon Felder said with a wide grin that made his gray mustache curl in the ends at the corners of his lips.

"Yes, my kids have everyone calling them that."

"Do you want anything, else?" Deacon Felder asked.

"No. Thanks."

Pastor Branford opened the door to his office, and the disarray of his own desk caught even him off guard. He had worked late into the night and had pulled out book after book from the shelves in his office to research a question he was asked during a counseling session. He was second guessing himself; after his meeting with Kitera Davidson. Looking at the desk also reminded him that he had tossed and turned all night wondering if his advice had been the best he could have offered.

One of his newer members had come to see him the day before. Her name was Kitera Davidson. Clarissa, Branford's secretary had left her membership profile on his desk for him to read before the appointment. Information in the file indicated that Kitera Davidson was thirty-nine, unmarried, and no children, employed as an office manager at a local business. Her initial interview with her Deacon indicated that Ms. Davidson had never belonged to any other church prior to joining Hope and Grace and had no other religious affiliations. She was taking the New Members classes and was a candidate for baptism. Kitera Davidson was assigned to Deacon Felder's New Members group. He had reported that she was attending New Members' classes regularly. Deacon Felder noted that she was attentive in class, completed all of her assignments and posed well thought out questions during class discussions of the material covered. She understood their concept of team work and agreed to their Small Group Ministry covenant which included a clause not to discuss information shared during their meetings outside of the group. Deacon Felder had not noted anything unusual in Ms. Davidson's profile that Branford felt he needed to be concerned about.

"Many new members have questions about becoming a part of a ministry or about sharing a gift or talent," Branford had thought, pulling out the information package on each of the church's ministries so that he could quickly and easily guide her to a ministry where she might fit in. He remembered patting himself on the back for how prepared he was for her visit.

Branford also pulled out some basic materials on effective prayer and a book on living life as a single Christian. He smiled to himself, "I am ready for Ms. Davidson" he thought. "I am finally getting good at this stuff. This will be my last meeting for the day. Clarissa is doing a great job with my schedule, 5:30PM meeting, 6:00PM finished, 6:30PM home in time for dinner with the family and everyone is happy," he said smugly to himself as he moved on to the rest of the days' business.

Chapter 3: Kitera

At exactly 5:15PM, Branford's secretary, Clarissa used her intercom to ring him. Clarissa announced, "Ms. Kitera Davidson, your 5:30PM appointment is waiting in the outer office."

"Please send her in," he responded. "5:15 meeting, 5:45 finished, 6:15 home for dinner," he adjusted his time line in his head while a self-satisfied smirk crept across his lips.

Clarissa opened the door to his office to allow Ms. Davidson in. Clarissa stuck her head in to say good night just before a particularly frail looking woman entered. She was dressed in droopy gray woolen slacks and a baggy maroon and gray striped sweater. She was pencil thin and the loose fitting clothes she was wearing did not help her looks at all. She was not carrying a handbag but carried a small red portfolio, and what he assumed was a Bible in a matching red canvas bag with a zipper going three quarters of the way around it.

Branford's thoughts went back to Kitera's profile that he had read earlier that morning. "Thirty-nine years old," he recalled the record saying. "Time has not been kind to her," he thought.

"Come in, please, Ms. Davidson. Here, have a seat." He motioned for her to take a seat in the black leather chair facing his desk.

"Thank you. Thank you for seeing me," she said. Her voice was much stronger than he had expected from her frail little body.

"Oh, my pleasure," he said and meant it.

"I see that you are attending our New Members' class. How have you found it so far?" Branford asked. Thinking to himself that a little small talk to help break the ice would help her to open up and speed things along, or at least he hoped that it would.

"Okay. So far I am really enjoying it and, please call me Kitera," she said.

"Sure," he replied.

"I've learned a lot in the class," she continued. "Many things that I wish I knew a long time ago." She paused for a moment seemingly hesitant about saying anything further.

Branford thought that he saw a tear but was not sure. He sat quietly for a moment to see if she wanted to continue her train of thought, but she said nothing further, so he sped ahead.

"I am glad that you are learning helpful things in the class. Deacon Felder says that you are one of his most attentive students" he said smiling. "You participate in class, ask questions and complete your reading and homework assignments. In fact, he has spoken very highly of you in our Team Leaders meetings."

"You talk about us in your meetings?" she said with a surprised look on her face.

"Sure, not the word-for-word conversation that takes place during your class. You don't have to worry about your teams' confidentiality agreement," he reassured her. "But I try to get to know our members through our leader's reports since I can't spend as much time with each member or family as I would like to. Tracking how well people do in our classes gives me some insight into what we are doing right and where we can improve. Your participation in the class benefits you, we hope and if it does then it should benefit the church, too. You see, I look at it like a circle."

Branford picked up a pen and began making circular doodles on the yellow pad lying in front of him on his desk as he talked. "I believe that the better you understand what the Bible teaches, the better you can serve God, and others. That is why we have taken great pains especially with our new members to get to know you through the New Members Class and to have you participate in other training and ministry opportunities. We want to get you off to a good start," he rattled on, thinking that he was unquestionably impressing the young women sitting before him with his pastoral prowess. He concluded his speech with, "Which brings me to the really important question of how I can be of service to you today?"

"I just wish that I had known about Christ a long time ago." Again, her eyes filled with tears. He was sure of it this time.

"That reaction is normal, Kitera, when people first come to accept Christ. All of us have some regrets in life. We are all human and make mistakes. Even after, we learn about Christ, we make mistakes; we do things that we regret.

"I know," she said.

The Pastor continued trying to be comforting, "We have done and may continue to do things that we are ashamed of; things that we know could not possibly please God. The good news is that each day that God gives us, is a day that we can ask for forgiveness for our sins. We, you, me, everyone who chooses too, can ask God to give us the courage and strength to do His will. Bradford felt as if he were rattling on too long. But he wanted to be certain that Kitera understood that he would not be judgmental, should she decide to open up to him about some problem that she was experiencing.

"I understand,' Kitera said.

Remember, the Bible tells us in 1 John 1:9, 'If we confess our sins, he is faithful and just and will forgive us our sins and purify us from all unrighteousness.' So don't worry about the past. Put those things behind you because they are forgiven and forgotten by God. Don't let your past cause you grief. Look forward and live the life God would have you live now. If you have asked for forgiveness then I am sure that God has not only forgiven you but forgotten the past," Branford concluded his rehearsed speech for situations such as this.

Again patting himself on the back and thinking to himself, "Great job, Rev. Branford." He was sure that he had handled himself well, "that should make her feel better."

Expecting Kitera to say thank you and be ready to leave his office with a smile on her face Branford was preparing to stand up, shake her hand, offer a brief prayer, and say good-bye when all of a sudden the flood gates opened and tears erupted out of Kitera's eyes like the water over Victoria Falls. A wail emitted from her throat that could have stopped a loaded freight train rolling at its top speed in its tracks. It startled Rev. Branford so badly he did not know if he should sit still or run. Her wail instantly shook him out of his self-congratulatory mood back into the real world.

A few seconds ticked by before Branford was able to close his mouth. Branford's first rational thought was, "Lord, I hope that I didn't say, 'Oh Crap,' out loud."

After a minute or two, Kitera's sobs stopped rocking her slender body, and she was finally able to grab a tissue from the box of Kleenex he was extending toward her.

All of the smugness Rev. Branford had exuded minutes earlier drained away as he asked almost timidly, "Kitera, can you tell me what's wrong?" He waited for a moment, but there was no discernible response from Kitera.

Branford took a deep breath and said, "Take your time. We don't have to rush," as he thought to himself, "Well, there goes dinner with the family tonight. No cursive writing for Penny, trouble,

trouble, trouble." Then, "Focus," he told himself. "Focus."

Kitera blew her nose several times. She made a soft sniffling noise trying hard to control the water works before she was actually able to get started with her story.

"My daughter, Daniela is dead," she said quietly. Her chest continued to heave up and down rapidly as she tried to get her breathing under control.

"I am so sorry to hear that," Branford said a little perplexed because there had been no mention of a daughter or any child for that matter in her profile. "How did we miss that?" he wondered to himself.

"I didn't realize that you had a child," Branford said.

"I didn't mention her when I filled out the member profile," Kitera said.

"Oh, I see," he said. "Do you mind if I ask why, not?"

"I don't like to talk about her."

"I'm sorry, I didn't mean to be intrusive," Branford said, not sure where to go with the conversation since she was the one who brought up her daughter.

"No you are not I'm, I am," she stuttered, "I'm just not sure if I am still considered a mother since my only child is dead. I just," she said, and her voice trailed off. Then she asked a question the pastor had no answer for, "What is the word for a mother who has lost her only child?"

"I'm not sure what you mean."

"When my husband died they called me a widow; a wife with a dead husband is no longer a wife. Right? She becomes a widow. So, a mother with no child is what? What name do they give her? What's her new title?"

Somewhat dumbfounded, Branford just looked at her without answering. The thought had never entered his mind before her question.

"If I had died," Kitera continued "the world would have called my daughter an orphan. But when a parent losses their only child, there is no word that I know of that expresses that state of being. No new status for your Facebook page. That is why I did not mention my child. What would I have said?" She asked as she shrugged her drooping shoulders.

Branford squirmed in his seat for a moment, swallowed hard then said, "I believe that, perhaps there is no word for a parent who has lost a child because your status as a parent has not changed. You are still a mother. Once you are a parent, you will always be a parent, as long as the memories of your child exist. Whether living or dead, you will always hold the love you have for your child in your heart. She will always be with you and you will always be her mother. If you ever have any doubt just think of the relationship between God the Father and God the Son. Remember that although the Son died on the cross there was no change in their relationship.

He was still the Son of God and God was still his Father. That relationship remained intact then and does even today. The same holds true for you."

Branford watched as Kitera stood slowly up from her chair.

"Excuse me," she said as she began to walk the few paces to the window. She stood at the window staring out of the window. She needed the pastor's soothing words to act like a balm being poured into the crevices of her mind where pain had taken up long-term residence.

Branford waited in silence for her to return to their conversation.

During their silent interlude, his response to Kitera's soul piercing questions caused the pastor to start thinking of writing a sermon based on her concerns about death and parenthood. He imagined himself in the pulpit announcing his sermon title, "Christ's status did not change in the grave; He was still the

Son of God. No," he thought, "I should make it more personal. The title should be, 'Your status will not change in the grave! But, the question is can you pass the paternity test?' Yeah that might preach." He scribbled notes on the pad in front of him.

Branford hurriedly searched his memory for a scripture that he could use to underscore the theme that believers were God's children, and would be so forever, on earth and in heaven. Quickly he settled on the words of John the Baptist about Jesus Christ found in John 1:12-13:

> Yet to all who did receive him, to those who believed in his name, he gave the right to become children of God— children born not of natural descent, nor of human decision or a husband's will, but born of God.

Branford's attention was drawn back to Kitera as he watched her try to deal with so much obvious emotional distress. Branford wondered to himself if he should consider adding a question on the *New*

Members Form that would allow a parent to indicate if their child was living or was deceased. This might encourage parents in Kitera's situation to feel good about acknowledging all of their children, not just the ones that were alive. He made more notes on his pad. His brainstorming was interrupted by Kitera's soft voice.

"Thank you," she whispered, drawing the preacher back into their conversation. She was already seated, in the chair, in front of him.

He forced himself to get his focus back on Kitera because he could still see so much anguish in her face. He looked directly into her eyes and said. "You mentioned that you are a widow."

"Yes, my husband was killed in a motorcycle accident when our daughter, Danni was a toddler. She did not remember him. It has just been the two of us, Danni and me since then."

"Do you have family in the area?" Branford asked, trying to get a feel for Kitera's support system.

"No, not really. Not anymore anyway. I moved to this area because of my husband. I found a good job here and even after my husband died I could provide a decent living for Danni and me, so I stayed. My mother came and stayed with me for a short while after my daughter died, but of course she eventually had to go home," she replied.

"Kitera, I can only begin to imagine your pain. I'm sorry for both of your losses. You have really been through a lot."

"Yes," she agreed as she shook her head up and down.

"I know that it must have been very painful for you to lose both your husband and your only child." Curious, Branford asked, "I know that you said, your husband died when your daughter was a toddler, but you did not say how long ago your daughter died. Did she die recently?"

"Yes. Well, no. I guess that it depends on what you consider recently. But it feels very recent to me. It was almost a year and a half ago now," she finally said.

She heaved another heavy sigh and sat back in the chair as if bracing for the possibility of another wave of tears.

"How old was she," he probed quickly hoping to stave off another crying spree.

"Sixteen. Only sixteen?"

"Was she ill or was it an accident?" he almost blurted out but decided it would be more appropriate to ask simply, "What happened?" instead.

"She was killed in a fight with her best friend," was a response Rev. Branford could never have anticipated.

"A fight with her best friend?" Branford repeated, making sure that he understood her clearly.

"Yes, her best friend, Diondra Davis." Kitera peered into the Pastor's eyes. She was trying to determine if he recognized the names, Diondra or Dean Davis. When there was no indication that he did, she continued softly. "I forgot that you have not been Pastoring here terribly long. It must have happened a few months before you came to Hope and Grace. All of the newspapers carried the story. My daughter Daniela, everybody called her Danni, and Diondra had been best friends since kindergarten. In fact, they met on their first day of kindergarten. Danni was a little nervous about her big first day of school. I decided to take her a little early and spend some time with her at the school to help calm her anxieties. Danni and I were standing in the playground area watching as the other children arrived. As it got closer to the time for me to leave, Danni got panicky about being left alone at the school, and began to cry.

Diondra noticed that she was crying and, came over. She introduced herself to us. 'Don't cry,' she said to Danni. 'My big "bother", Dean goes here. He says that there are lots of fun things to do. We can go to the library, and the computer lab. We will even have lunch in the cafeteria like the older kids. Don't you think that's cool?"

"I guess," Danni said showing a little curiosity in what her new friend had to say.

Thankful for the distraction, I asked Diondra, "Didn't you mean big brother?"

"No, he is a big bother," Diondra said emphatically, and we all laughed.

"He calls me his 'little cyst' instead of little sister. He thinks that I don't know what it means, but I do."

"What's does it mean?" Danni asked her.

Diondra gave Danni a five-year-olds explanation of a cyst. Then Diondra talked non-stop. By the time the bell rang, Danni was calm and ready to go into class by herself.

"Really, that must have made you feel good.'

"Yes, it did."

"Diondra was always more mature than Danni, although their birthdays were only three months apart. From that day on Diondra sort of took Danni under her wing. Danni was so happy when she found out that Diondra was in her same kindergarten class. Over the years Diondra came to be more like a big sister to Danni than a friend. The next morning, Danni was rushing me to take her to school because she wanted to play with her new friend, Diondra before class started. Later, because their names were so similar, they were in the same homerooms in Middle and High School. They also took many of the same AP classes, too. They were practically inseparable. My Danni loved Diondra like a sister and vise-versa. The girls were more like twins than friends. When Danni wasn't at Diondra's house, Diondra was at ours.

They played on the same softball team, Danni was the pitcher and Diondra was the catcher. They both swam on the high school swim team. Danni was better at the 200 meter, but Diondra usually won every 100 meter race they competed in. We, Diondra's parents and I called them the Dynamic Duo. Our families even went on vacations together most summers, because the girls would have it no other way. Danni, like I said, was an only child, and I was so happy that she had a friend like Diondra, someone to hang out with, to kind of grow up with. You know what I mean?"

"Yes," he nodded his head in agreement.

"As a parent, it made my life easier because I knew that I always could trust Diondra's parents with my precious baby, and I always treated Diondra as if she were my own child." Kitera declared shaking her head slowly as if she could see Danni and Diondra in front of her at that very instant.

As Branford sat staring at the distraught woman facing him, he remembered his earlier comment to himself about time having not been kind to her. He was ashamed of his thoughtlessness even though he had only said it to himself. "What happened to them?" he asked. "Why were they fighting?"

"It was a boy," she blurted out.

"A boy?" Branford repeated.

"Yes," she said understanding the suspicious tone of her Pastor's voice. "But not just any boy, she hurriedly added. It was Diondra's brother, Dean."

Like an echo, Branford repeated, "Diondra's brother? But why? Why would they fight over her brother?"

"That is what I could not understand at first, either."

"Did you find out?"

'Oh, yes, I went to see Diondra as soon as I could after the accident. I couldn't believe what I was being told. I needed to hear it from Diondra's own lips."

"That must have been painful."

"Yes, but I needed to do it. So when, Carla, Diondra's mother called me and said that Diondra wanted to see me, I had to go. In fact, she said that Diondra begged her to ask me to come. She wanted me to know that what happened was an accident. She said that she would never hurt Danni on purpose. She was devastated by the whole thing. Her whole family was devastated."

Branford interrupted, Kitera for just a moment, "I am sorry Kitera, but you said accident just now but before I thought you said she was killed in a fight."

"Yes, I know, you will understand in a minute. You see, Diondra says that on the afternoon that it happened she and Danni were in the locker room of the high school gymnasium getting changed for softball practice like always. She was already in her catcher's gear when she noticed that Danni had barely started to get dressed. 'Get a move on Danni; we don't want to be late. We will have to run laps,' she had said to Danni. But Danni continued to sit on the bench without moving. So she asked, 'Danni, is anything wrong?'"

'My stomach feels queasy,' Danni had replied. Kitera pressed her intertwined fingers to her tummy as if she could feel Danni's pain.

"Diondra said she asked, 'Still? You said that this morning, too. Maybe it is some kind of bug. Do you want me to tell the coach? Do you want to go to the nurse?'"

"'No,' Danni had said. 'I don't think it's a bug or anything.'"

"Diondra asked again, 'Are you sure you don't want me to get someone?'"

'No, I'll be okay.'

'Are you going to come out? You know you might feel better once you get outside and get loosened up.'

'I don't think so,' Danni had said. Then she asked Diondra a question that Diondra thought was strange. 'Di, if I did something terrible would you still be my best friend?'

Diondra said that she thought she meant quitting softball or something like that, so she said, 'Girl don't you know that you can't do anything so terrible that I wouldn't be your friend? Remember the promise we wrote in each other's Jr. High year books, 'Best buds for life.' Nothing has changed for me, how about for you?'

'No, nothing has changed for me either. I want to tell you something, Di, but I am scared.'

'Scared, why would you be scared? Just spit it out. Whatever it is we will work it out. Nothing is bad enough to make yourself sick over.'

"Diondra said that Danni just sat looking at her, so she asked, "Is your mom thinking about moving again? I promise that I will beg my Mom and Dad to let you move in with us until we graduate and go off to college together, just like we planned. You know they love you, too? Right? It won't be a problem. We can fix whatever it is. You know how relentless I am when I want to get my way. Remember Disney World? Come on, get dressed Danni, don't worry it will be okay.""

'No,' Danni had said. 'It is nothing like that. Please, just sit down here beside me and listen to me for a minute.'

So Diondra said that she sat next to Danni on the bench and Danni moved very close to her and whispered softly because she did not want anyone else to hear. 'Di, I think I might be pregnant.'

'No,' Diondra had said, jumping off of the bench and facing Danni shaking her head like she had not understood what was being said.

'Di, sit down, please,' a soft but strong order had come from Danni's lips, which Diondra had obediently followed.

When she sat back down Diondra said 'But, Danni that's not possible. You don't have a boyfriend.

Danni didn't respond she just looked at her. So she got upset because she thought that maybe Danni had been raped or something.

She asked, "Danni, did someone hurt you? You can tell me if they did. I swear, Danni I'll make the person pay."

"No, nothing like that, Di."

"But, you haven't even mentioned being with a boy, Danni. We see each other every day, and you never said anything before today."

"I know, I just could not tell you before now. Please don't be mad."

"I am not mad, Danni, and I am listening to you, but I don't get it. You are not making any sense. You haven't had time to be with a boy. I mean, between school, practice, homework; you hardly have enough time to sleep. Besides that our parents are like drill sergeants. They never let us go anywhere unless they know in advance where it is, who's going, who's driving. Plus they still have big bother, Dean watching over us like a guard dog. She said that she expected Danni to laugh like she always did when they called Dean "big bother" but she didn't. So Diondra just said, 'You must be confused.'"

"I am not, Di believe me. I wish that I was, but I am not."

"Danni," Diondra said, "if you missed your period maybe it's because you have been exercising too much or something. You may just be irregular you know.

'Diondra, please listen.'

'I am listening, but I know that we tell each other everything and you never said anything about being with no boy. You must be mistaken. Do you have a fever? I believe that you are sick, honestly I do, but maybe it is just a bug.'

'Di, hear me out, please,' Danni had said as she took Diondra's hand. 'I should have told you that I was seeing someone before, but I was afraid you would be mad at me and that I might have to choose between you and the person I love.'

'What kind of craziness are you talking about? Choosing between me your best friend and some boy you love? Come on give me a break. Why would you seeing someone matter that much to me? Why would you have to choose? If you found, someone you truly like I would be happy for you. Look, this is my happy face, she had said, and she pulled the corners of her lips up to make a face at Danni. She was still trying to get her to laugh, but Danni was too serious.

'Stop kidding Di, please.'

'Okay, I just want you to see that I am glad that you like someone. Really, I am if it is true, but I still don't believe that you are pregnant.'

'Di, would you still be happy for me if the boy I'm seeing were Dean?'

'Dean, who?' Diondra asked. Danni grabbed her hand and squeezed it tight but did not answer.

Kitera continued the story. "Diondra said, 'My brother? Dean? Oh, so you are just kidding. Is it April Fool's Day? Did I miss something? You had me fooled for a minute. I was buying the whole story, hook, line and sinker, as my grandfather would say. Except for the pregnant part you really had me going. Come on stop fooling around, let's go. I don't want to run laps because of this craziness.'"

Branford listened as Kitera relayed the story just as Diondra had told it to her.

"Diondra was about to stand up when Danni said, 'Di, stop, I am not kidding. I do think I am pregnant, and it is Dean's baby.' She said it in a muffled voice Diondra said. Then Danni looked her straight in the face."

For the first time, Diondra saw the look on her friend's face and knew that she was telling the truth. 'There were tears in Danni's eyes,' Diondra told me." Kitera moved on retelling the story as if Diondra was whispering it in her ear.

"Diondra said she got angry. She felt angrier than she ever remembered being in her whole life. She felt betrayed by Danni and Dean. Lied to, used, just downright hurt. How could they have done this she thought? She stood up and began to walk away. She wanted to get as far away from Danni as she could possibly get. She wanted to find Dean and ask him what was going on. She wanted to know if what Danni was saying was true. She needed some air, some time to think things over. She slammed her locker door closed and had taken another few steps when Danni came up behind her and grabbed her jersey. 'Wait,' Danni cried. 'Wait, wait. Don't just walk away from me, please, Di. I need you.'

"Diondra says that she spun around and looked Danni in the face and said, 'I hate you. Keep your nasty hands off of me.' And with that she pushed Danni away with all of her might. Danni lost her balance and fell backwards. She hit the base of her neck on the bench they had been sitting on. The bench was screwed into the floor and did not give an inch when Danni's neck hit it. Her neck snapped. Her C3 vertebra was severed. She regretted pushing Danni immediately. She didn't intend to hurt her; she just wanted to get away from her to sort things out. She realized quickly that Danni was hurt. Diondra said that she was hysterical begging Danni to get up, apologizing to her for pushing her but Danni couldn't move. Danni was looking around Diondra said, like she didn't understand what was happening. The last thing that she understood Danni to say was "tell my Mom." She didn't know if Danni wanted her to tell me what happened, or to tell me that she was pregnant or something else. Danni never finished the sentence. The coach said she was dead within a few minutes. She was gone before the paramedics arrived.

With one angry push, Diondra killed my baby girl and my grandchild. Sometimes, I wish she had killed me too. I know that she didn't mean to do it, but Danni is still dead."

"I am so sorry," was all Rev. Branford could think of to say as he tried to take all that she had said in.

Kitera was silent for a moment then said, "It is okay. I'm dealing with that pain and the loss okay now. I've even forgiven Diondra and Dean."

"Yes, but I can see that it is still be hard for you to deal with your feelings about your daughter's death," Branford said thinking of how Kitera had cried as she began to tell him about her daughter.

"You are right," she agreed.

"What happened to Diondra after the accident?" He asked "She must have been shattered."

"Yes, in fact, both Diondra and Dean had emotional problems afterwards. They both blamed themselves for Danni's death."

"Really?"

Yes, Dean may have been the worse of the two. He tried to take his own life because of the guilt. Thank God he was unsuccessful. It was too much for him, the loss of Danni, his unborn son, his sister's arrest and the newspaper reporters hounding him and his family night and day. It was just too much."

"I can understand that. So, your daughter was pregnant?"

"Yes, about four months. She was caring a little boy."

"And the girl, Diondra, she went to jail?"

"Yes, she was arrested."

"Did anyone else know that Danni was pregnant before that day?" What he honestly wanted to know is if she knew that her daughter was pregnant before all of this happened.

"No. No one had any idea. I certainly did not. She wasn't showing or anything and with sports and all of her other activities her period had always been kind of irregular. I didn't notice anything."

"Not even Dean?"

"No, he did not know either. It was as much of a surprise to him as it was to Diondra and the rest of us."

"Did you have any idea that Dean and Danni were seeing each other?"

No, none of us had any idea that Dean and Danni were seeing each other. We didn't even suspect that they thought of each other in that way. I mean they were always friends, and when Dean got his driver's license he became sort of a designated chauffeur for the girls - taking them to and from games, school, the movies, just regular stuff. We all, his parents and I just assumed that he and Danni felt like brother and sister. They basically grew up together, so we trusted them to be alone together. I trusted him with Danni, and his parents trusted Danni with him. We threw them together without ever considering teenage hormones and the possibility that they could be attracted to each other. We all made mistakes that Danni paid for unnecessarily with her life and Dean nearly paid for with his."

Rev. Branford and Kitera were both silent for a moment, recounting the story details in their minds and thinking of all of the other possible outcomes.

"I know that it might sound strange," she continued, "but I still love Diondra and Dean. So much of our lives were interwoven, and we shared so much pain together over the loss of Danni that I could not help but continue to love them. I know that what happened to Danni was an accident. I don't believe for a moment that Diondra meant to hurt her. She just reacted. I was beside myself with anger too when I first heard that Danni was pregnant. I don't know how I would have reacted, and I am an adult. Of course, I don't believe that I would have hurt her, but I might have wanted some alone time before I would have been able to talk with her about it. I don't know. I know that Diondra is just a child herself. She simply reacted before she thought things through."

"I get that part. Still, it has to be hard for you to accept."

Yes, I it was hard for me to accept that Danni and Dean had been lovers, and that they had kept it from everyone. But, I also know that Danni would have wanted us to continue to love each other. It was just a crazy accident. But I didn't feel that way in the beginning, though."

"Well, after speaking with you, I can say that you do seem to be handling that part of your life uncommonly well, Kitera."

"Now, maybe, but at first I wanted to hurt Diondra, Dean and their entire family. I wanted to strike out at everybody; even my mother and I did initially.

'Really?'

"Yes. I thank God that my mother was sympathetic, and she understood the reasons for my bad attitude and behavior."

"What happened?"

"My mother was trying to help me with the funeral arrangements because I was a complete mess. Even though, I was glad for her help, when my mother offered to look in Danni's closet for a dress, I went ballistic on her. She only wanted to see if there was something in the closet that Danni could be buried in. You see, I had not been in Danni's room since she died and I did not want anyone else to go in there either. I didn't want her to move anything. I wanted everything to stay just the way it had been the day she left for school. I could not accept that she was not coming home, that thought seemed just too unreal to me during that time. But my mother just held me and let me cry it out."

"I am sure that she understood that you were not angry at her but at the situation."

"Yeah, she did. She was there for me through everything."

"I am glad to hear that you had help when you needed it."

Chapter 4: The Diary

The skies darkened, and time passed swiftly while Pastor Branford and Kitera talked about the events that followed her daughter's death. From his window, he could see the solar lights in the church parking lot come on. The glistening light shone down on a dwindling number of parked cars, but the growing lateness of the hour did not impede their conversation. Kitera was eager now to tell her story, and the Pastor was a willing and spellbound listener. "Danni wanted me to know something that day," Kitera said with her emotions clearly in check. "She told Diondra to tell me something, but she never got to say what it was."

"You mean after she was pushed?"

"Yes, it haunted me for a long time. I wanted to know what it was that she wanted me to know. I thought maybe she wanted me to know that she was sorry or maybe to say that she loved me. Maybe she wanted me to know about the baby, all of those scenarios crossed my mind when Diondra told me that Danni's last words 'were tell my Mom.' No one was certain what she wanted me to know. There were too many variables, too many things that she could have wanted me to know. So many questions were unanswered. I agonized over that for a while. She was not calling for me like that baby that I thought of her as; instead she was trying to let me know something, maybe that she was a young woman. A young woman that I would never get to know, carrying a baby that I would never get to hold. She was teary again"

"I can understand your frustration." He said as he handed her the tissue box.

"Thank you."

The pastor nodded his head.

"But, now that I found Danni's diaries, I realized that what she wanted me to know is probably what she says in the diary. The answer was there all of the time, I believe. Danni's messages to me from the grave I call them. I can hear her speaking to me so clearly in them."

"Her diaries," Branford repeated.

"Yes. This will probably sound crazy, but I am going to tell you anyway."

"I'm listening."

"One night I was sitting on the sofa, feeling sort of sorry for myself, when I heard Danni's voice as clear as a bell. "'Diary' was the one word she spoke."

"What?" the Pastor said as he raised his brow, shaking his head.

"It was like she was reaching out to me from her grave. It was as if she was sending me a message or maybe finishing her sentence, "Tell my, Mom." She

71

had left me notes, and she reminded me about them from her grave."

"And what happened?" Rev. Branford asked.

"I jumped up and ran to her room looking for the diaries. Before that night, I could hardly bear to go into her room. But that night I was all over her room. I was looking through every diary that she had ever kept. She and Diondra would exchange diaries as gifts each Christmas. Danni would mark the year on the outside. Then she would place the old dairy in a beat-up old trunk that she kept in her room. She called the trunk her treasure chest. She kept pictures, birthday money, report cards, and all kinds of memorabilia in it."

"Did she talk about the pregnancy in the diary?"

"Yes, she did. I found her most recent diary, but I could not find the key. So, I took it to the kitchen and picked at the lock with a knife until it opened and I began to read it. Danni wrote in her diary almost every night. I teased her often about it by calling her our family historian because she could look in her diary for the date of almost anything significant that had happened in her life."

"I understand my oldest daughter keeps a diary, too. It is off limits to everybody," Branford said with a half-smile.

"Yeah, Danni was the same way."

"So, you were able to get some clarity about what happened between her and Dean by reading her diary?"

"Yes. About a year before this all happened, Danni, Diondra and Dean participated in a local cotillion. Diondra's mother and I thought that it would be a great way for the kids to learn proper etiquette, good table manner and things like that."

Branford nodded as Kitera recounted the story, encouraging her to go on.

"We were probably more excited about the program than the kids were, but they eventually got into it, and everything went well. The girls didn't have boyfriends, so that made it easy to have Danni and Dean go as partners, and Diondra went with one of her cousins. In her diary, Danni wrote that during practice Dean was exciting to be with. He was funny, polite and easy to talk to. The kids were paired off like couples. They spent time together learning dances, eating, doing little projects. After a while it all seemed exceedingly romantic to her. She wrote that it was during the classes leading up to the cotillion that she first began to think of Dean as something other than Diondra's pesky older "bother". He was becoming her special friend. On the night of the cotillion she says that she was sad that everything was coming to an end. She wrote that she told Dean that she liked him and that she wanted to go out with him. She was hurt when he turned her down flat.

"Really?" Surprised, the pastor asked. "He turned her down."

"Yes, but a few days later she says that they talked about it again. She told Dean that she missed hanging out with him. He said that he missed hanging out with her, too. So, they decided to give their new relationship a try. She was so very happy about that, and she did not even trust me enough to share that with me."

"Sorry," the pastor said trying to console Kitera.

"No, it's okay." Kitera said with a half-smile. "They agreed to keep their relationship a secret, in case things did not work out. Danni and Dean agreed that it would be better that way until they knew for sure exactly how they felt about each other.

"Did she say why?"

"They didn't want any negative fallout in case things did not work out. If only the two of them knew about it, they could act like nothing ever happened, and no one would be the wiser."

"I see, makes sense, I suppose," said Branford.

"But, I could tell from her writing that she was happy and excited. She even pasted a picture in the diary of herself and Dean from the cotillion. She drew hearts all around the border and colored them all in red. They looked cute together, a smile crossed her face. In the picture, she was in her white ball gown, and he was in his tuxedo. Her introduction to proper society isn't that what the cotillion is supposed to be. Proper society," she repeated.

Kitera stopped for a moment then continued. "After that, she wrote about innocent things like how Dean helped her with algebra. Or how Dean helped her with her pitching and bat swinging techniques. She wrote how she was glad that no one seemed to notice the change in her and Dean's relationship," Kitera said shrugging her shoulders.

"Most of what she wrote was benign teenage stuff, game schedules, library book due dates, that kind of thing."

"I see," Branford said.

"She talked about them meeting at the library, sneaking a kiss or holding hands when Diondra wasn't around."

"Did she ever say how she and Dean came to sleep together?"

"Yes, eventually she wrote about sneaking into Dean's room one night that she spent with Diondra. She didn't say if he asked her to or if she decided to do it on her own, but it was obvious that it was something that she wanted to do."

"About two months later she even wrote a note to herself to remember to add sanitary napkins to the grocery shopping list so that I would not become suspicious about her missed periods."

"And she never said anything to anyone?"

"No."

"Poor baby", Branford said

"I know, she considered having an abortion but changed her mind. She even considered running away because she thought that I would be so disappointed in her that I would not want her around," she said as a shallow river of tears trickled down her cheek again. She halted for a moment.

"It's okay. Take your time," Said Branford.

"The night before the accident she wrote that she was going to confide in Diondra that she was going to be an aunt. She wrote Auntie Di all over the page. She hoped that Diondra would help her to tell Dean and everyone else about the pregnancy. She wanted Diondra to help her. She never dreamed that Diondra would hurt her. No one could have imagined that Diondra would cause her death. I can't even believe it today." It took a few seconds for Kitera to absorb the painful thoughts.

She pulled a few small pieces of crumpled paper from the red leather bag where Pastor Branford assumed she kept her Bible. Then she said something that struck Branford as most unusual.

"Danni even wrote about praying the night before she died for the first time." Kitera began reading from one of the sheets of paper: 'Dear Diary, Today was the first time I ever tried praying to God. I don't know if I did it right or if the Jesus I hear people talking about is real. I sure hope that he is because I know that I need all of the help I can get to make it through this. I hope that he will help me. So, I didn't think that it would hurt if I prayed.'

"Really?" the Pastor asked as he made a mental note in preparation for the question of where Danni would spend eternity. He reminded himself that the subject usually worked its way into the conversation when parents had lost unsaved children. Be prepared, he told himself, if, not today, certainly sometime in the future, he was sure that he would be asked the question, "Where did Danni go when she died?" His thoughts swiftly returned to what Kitera was saying.

"Yes, Kitera began reading again, 'God, maybe you will have pity on me and will help me if that is possible. I am sorry for all of the trouble I have caused. More than anything else, I hope everyone will forgive me and that my friendship with Di is strong enough to survive this. I wish that I had told Di before now that Dean and I were seeing each other. But now it is too late to ask her what she thinks or how my being with Dean would make her feel. Now that, I am pregnant it is too late to ask. Why did I let this happen? I need her friendship, but I don't know if she will want to be friends. I want to share everything with her, like we always do. I've never kept any secrets from her before this. I need her. I know that if Di is on my side, it will make everything else easier, but telling her will be the hardest thing I have ever had to do.' Kitera folded the paper back up and put it away.

Later she wrote, 'We had so many dreams, and now maybe they won't come true. Dean will worry that he won't be able to go to college. He will probably feel like I ruined his life. I don't know what I will do if everybody hates me. I just don't know what I'll do. If Diondra or my mother hates me, I will just want to die. What if Dean feels like I messed up his life? I couldn't stand that. He has to know that I never meant to do anything to hurt him. I wanted to make him happy; instead I have probably lost him forever. Why didn't I think about all of this before I slept with Dean? I never meant to hurt anyone. I am sorry. Please God, if you can, please help me and my baby. I love all of them, my mother, Diondra, Dean, even their parents. I wish that I could wake up and find that this was all just a dream and that everything was back to normal. I hope that tomorrow after everything is over that my Mom will just give me a big hug and say 'it's okay'", was the last thing she wrote."

"Danni sounds like a great kid. It seems that she was really sorry for the mistake that she made. She was obviously concerned about you and how you might react. I am sure that she did not want to disappoint you because she loved you.

"I know, and I would have been disappointed, but we could have gotten through it. All she had to do was to come to me. I would have done just what she wanted. I would have given her a big hug and told her that everything was going to be okay."

"I know. You know what, you are right, it does sound almost like a note to you from Danni from the grave, a messages to help ease your mind. You are more blessed than many people because you have a written record in her own words of her thoughts about the things that were important to her," the pastor told her, "considering how many people don't know what their kids are thinking, and they live under the same roof."

"Yes, if only I had known what she was thinking when she was living, maybe this would never have happened. I always thought that we had a great relationship and that she knew she could come to me with any problem she had, but when it mattered most, she was afraid."

"Maybe it was not so much fear of you, but shame," Rev. Branford interjected. "Most young people are impulsive and do things they later regret. Nobody likes to face the music when they recognize the possible consequences, especially in a situation like this. For a teenager, it must seem like an almost impossible task."

"Yes, but it would have been easy for me to understand what happened if she had only talked to me. Not that she was blameless in this situation, but every place you look someone is telling not just young people but everybody that having sex is okay and that it does not matter if you are married or not or if you are married that it doesn't matter if it is with your wife or husband or not. Commercials for everything from milk to chewing gum say 'use us and become sexy.' Almost every movie even the ones supposedly made for kids includes some unnecessary sex scene in it. Take this pill for better sex, if you watch TV or read a book or ride down a highway you would believe that everything on earth was centered on sex. It is crazy."

"I agree with you," Rev. Branford said.

"I should have been more vigilant. I should have talked to her more about her feelings and her body. I should have noticed some sign of a change in her."

"Even parents can't see and know everything."

"Yes, but I prided myself on knowing her and giving her everything that I thought she needed. I failed her."

"I am sure that you tried your best."

"That is just it, now I know that I did not give her the one thing, maybe the only real thing that she needed: a God to believe in. She wore designer jeans, had brand named everything, and every gadget she asked for, I tried to get, you name it, but never once did I think to offer her, Christ. I never thought that it was important for her to have the name, Christian. I would think of taking her to Sephora to shop for Christian Dior before I would think to bring her to church in search of Christ. In the end, she was looking for God on her own. She needed Christ, and I took her to swimming lessons on Sunday mornings instead of Sunday School. We had Christmas but no Christ. I gave her gifts that she left behind to haunt me. It seems that memories and regrets are all I have left. .

"Regrets?"

Yes, regrets. Now that it is too late. I realize that I needed to give her so much more. Something that may have helped her fight the temptations to be with Dean. Maybe she would still be alive if I had." She said and paused for a moment. "Deacon Felder had us memorize a few verses from, Psalm 119 in our New Members class. The first time we read the verses I had to excuse myself from class because I was afraid that I would not be able to control my emotions.

"I know the verses you mean; it's about young people, right?" Branford asked.

Yes, verse 9 essentially asks the question, 'How can a young person stay on the path of purity? The answer it says is by living according to God's word. Verse 10 says, 'I seek you with all my heart; do not let me stray from your commands. I have hidden your word in my heart that I might not sin against you.' I never bothered to teach Danni God's Word. I never thought of her as a person with a soul that needed to be saved. She was a child with her whole life ahead of her or so, I thought.

"I, know" Branford said. "Most people see children that way." He stopped short of saying what he was really thinking, that even he had not felt a genuine urgency to see the souls of children saved. When he thought of ministering to children, the words fun and exciting were more likely to come to mind than salvation. He wanted the workers in the Children's Ministry of Hope and Grace to focus on making sure that the kids have a good time, make them want to come back, he told his staff. That way, maybe their parents will get involved with the church. He was beginning to see that his idea of children's ministry was more of a marketing strategy than anything else. The souls of the children had not been a first priority. He had not looked at the children and asked, 'where will you spend eternity?' not even his own children. His first question after Sunday School or Children's Church to Penny, Jai and even Abigail was did you have fun. He never asked, 'Did you accept Christ.' At least, until now it had been that way, he thought. I could kick myself.

Kitera continued, "What chance did Danni have to stay pure or to live the life God wanted for her? She will never have the chance to live the life her father would have wanted for her, the life I wanted for her or even the life she wanted for herself."

In a sense, I sent her into the world with only her own instincts to guide her. There was no God in her life except maybe on the next to her last day, and it was too late then. There were no rules other than my own and the ones she made for herself. There were no guidelines for living a good and decent Christian life. As a parent, I should have done better by her. I would never have said, 'Oh, she will learn how to cross the street by herself, when she is a little older and left her on her own to face traffic. No, I took the time to tell her to look both ways before she crossed the street. Cross at the corner. Don't cross in the middle of the block. But about life, I didn't tell her to be careful because many of the things that the world encourages you to do are not right or good for you. I didn't tell her that Jesus was unquestionably her best friend, not Diondra, Dean or even me. She should have had no doubts that He would forgive her even if no one else ever did," tears once again glistened in Kitera's eyes. "It seems so harsh that I can't undo this, now that I know better, now that I understand what I did was wrong."

"Kitera, listen. There is not one parent alive who, if honest with themselves, could not look back at how they raised their children and see many things that they could have done better or would change if they had the opportunity. None of us has that power though, which is why it is crucial for us to keep our minds on what God is doing in our lives in the present. How can God use us today?" he said looking straight into her bleary eyes. "I know that you know that I'm right," he said smiling at her.

"Besides that, you don't really know what Danni's real relationship was with God, except that she was at very least seeking Him and asking for help. She knew enough about Christ to at least hope that what she had heard was true. She knew enough to at least do that. Right."

"You are right," she said. "I hate to admit it, but I guess that there were a lot of things that I did not know about my daughter and never will."

"No parent ever does." Branford said trying to be encouraging.

"Thank you," she said again. This time there was a faint smile on Kitera face.

Still not genuinely understanding the purpose for the meeting, Rev. Branford sat back a little in his chair and tried to organize his choice of words carefully before inquiring again, "Kitera, you seem to have put things in their proper perspective about Danni's accident but, you seemed very upset when you began talking about your daughter's death. Is there something else about the situation that is bothering you? Did something happen recently to upset you?"

"Yes, there is," she said in a matter of fact manner. "Because the fight occurred on school grounds, if you can call it a fight, Diondra was arrested. The newspapers played up the fact that Danni was pregnant. It was front page news, 'Pregnant Teen Murdered in High School Brawl.' Everyone close to either family knows that it was an accident. Diondra would not have intentionally hurt Danni except under those extreme circumstances. Even then, I don't believe she meant to hurt her. It was a split second reaction that caused a terrible mistake, an accident. But she was arrested and charged with the crime. I believe that she could have proven at a trial that it was an accident, but Diondra's parents did not think she was stable enough to go through a trial at the time and with Dean trying to commit suicide…" her voice trailed off slightly, "I don't think any of them would have made it through a trial very well. So, Diondra finally was allowed to plead guilty to a reduced charge and is scheduled to go for a sentencing next Monday."

Rev. Branford leaned in with both elbows propped on his desk, and his face clasped in his hands, listening carefully for the nexus of the reason of the visit to be revealed.

Kitera opened her leather portfolio and pulled out a small notebook and began to read over some notes before she began talking. "Rev. Branford," she said as if she had practiced asking the question before. "During New Members' Class when we discussed eternal salvation we were told that in order to be saved a person must accept Christ as their personal Savior. Deacon Felder said that if we accept Christ as our Savior, he will act as an intercessor for us before God asking that our sins be forgiven and that when we die we will receive the gift of eternal life. Is that correct?" she asked.

"Yes," Rev. Branford replied.

"Over the last six months I have accepted Christ as my Savior, confessed my sins and asked forgiveness of them, and I will be baptized soon."

"Yes, I know," said Rev. Branford.

"Well, Carla, Diondra' mother has asked me to make a statement at the sentencing hearing on Diondra's behalf. She wants me to ask the judge to give Diondra probation instead of time in jail. She has asked me to tell the judge that I don't want Diondra punished any further."

"How do you feel about that?"

"I would like to do that accept for the fact that I keep thinking that because of Diondra, my baby may be condemned to Hell, never having been given the opportunity to accept Christ as her Savior. She said in her diary that she did not know if Jesus was real. Doesn't that mean that she will go to hell?"

Although, he had anticipated the question, he was not ready for it. Rev. Branford could feel his own eyes begin the burn and fill with tears as he watched a slithery stream of water float down the face of this woman in palpable agony sitting in front of him.

"You see," she continued. "I was not raised in a Christian home. I knew very little about Christ or God or church, and I did not bring or even send my daughter to church ever. To be honest, I did not see a need for it. Like I said before, I always thought that religion would be one of those things Danni would learn about when she grew up and that she would make up her mind about it when she was old enough to understand it. I don't believe Danni had ever been inside a church before she died. Her funeral was even at the funeral home not a church.

"I don't think I am alone in this," she continued. "Most parents assume that their children will grow up and will outlive them. I did not plan on burying my child or learning too late about things that I should have done for her and with her as a child. If I had believed in Christ earlier, or had some kind of relationship with God before now, I would have told her. But now," she stuttered. "Now it is too late" She finally got it out.

"And the thought of her in hell, is hell to me." Her voice grew louder with each word she spoke. "So the thought of begging for forgiveness of the person who caused her to go there is unconscionable to me right now. Even though, in my heart of hearts I know it is the right thing to do, I don't believe that I can do it."

"Diondra" she continued, "will have an opportunity to accept Christ."

"Her family did not attend church either, I take it."

"No, Carla and Andrew, Diondra and Dean's parents own a restaurant. They both worked most week-ends. So, Diondra spent many of them with us, Danni and me. I feel some guilt about her, too. I had every opportunity to take them to church, but I never did." Kitera sighed and said "In fact, I feel guilty about a lot of things."

"Such as?"

"Diondra can still be saved, even though she caused Danni's death. Danni will never have that chance. Help me, please to understand this so that I can live with myself. I want to help Diondra, but I feel like I will be betraying Danni if I do. It seems that no matter what decision I make it will be the wrong one." Kitera had spoken the last words with a trembling, pleading voice, but they sounded like thunder to her pastor.

Rev. Branford folded his hands and brought them under his chin, closed his eyes and silently prayed a very humble prayer: "Lord, I am not sure of what to say or do – but I know that you know exactly what is needed. So I ask that you use me as your instrument. Speak through me. Give me the right answers to the questions being asked of me. Help to ease the pain of whatever decision might be made here today or in the coming days regarding this situation. In Jesus' name, I pray. Amen." When he opened his eyes, he saw Kitera staring curiously at him.

"You are indeed faced with what might be a heart wrenching decision for some and I am in awe of your forgiving spirit and your compassion for Diondra and her brother Dean. I know that it takes a very loving, kind and generous woman to forgive not one person but two individuals who caused the death of their child, though unintentional as it may have been. You are a blessing to me, and I am so very proud to call you my sister in Christ," he said with emotion in his voice.

"You are wrestling with a decision that no mother would choose to have to make - to ask forgiveness and leniency on the young woman who killed your beloved child under any circumstances would be difficult but to have her taken at such a young age is an absolute tragedy. First, let me say to you that God has the last say on who will be saved and who will not.

"The Bible tells us that God knows us even before we are formed in our mother's wombs. He knows everything about us even before we are born. Do you remember the story of Samson in the book of Judges? Most people know about Samson and Delilah, how she tricked him in to telling her the secret of his strength which led to his being captured by his enemies. You do remember that part, right?

"Yes," she answered, waiting he was sure for some astute revelation.

Did you know that before Samson was born an angel revealed to his mother that he was going to be a special child, a Nazirite, which was a person who was consecrated to God? The angel gave Samson's mother instructions that she had to follow even before he was born. He told her not to drink any wine or any other fermented drink and not to eat anything unclean because the boy would be a Nazirite from birth. So we know that God knew him before he was born, and he knows all of us before we are born including, Danni."

Kitera shook her head yes although she was not quite sure what the pastor was talking about. "Didn't he realize that her daughter was dead? What did this have to do with anything," she wondered but she nodded her head yes hoping that he would move on quickly.

"Yes, I understand that for me, now, but it doesn't help me to decide what to do about Diondra."

Trying to make it clear to Kitera that God knows all about each person and has a plan for their lives, even if that life ends early in our human way of thinking, Branford moved on, "Do you mind if I ask how you came to Hope and Grace? Were you invited by a member of the church or did you find out about our church from our website? How did you first come to know about Hope and Grace?

"I was invited by Thelisa McManus. She works with me, and she invited me."

"Okay, I know Thelisa. How long have you worked with her?"

"I've worked with her for about seven years. After Danni died, I was a wreck like I said, and Thelisa began to talk to me at lunch. At first she would just ask how I was doing. After a while, she began to talk to me about Christ. She asked me if I was a believer. I did not know what she meant at first, and I wasn't too interested when I learned that she meant a believer in Christ. But talking with her did help me get through my work day so I would listen. Later, we started to read the bible together. In time, she asked me if I wanted to accept Christ as my Savior. I said yes, and we prayed together for Him to come into my life sitting at a table in the cafeteria. Afterward, she invited me to come to church with her, and I agreed to come. When I got here, I found that I enjoyed being around the members. They were friendly, and didn't seem to judge me when I would ask questions that had to seem stupid to them since I knew so little about what worship was about. I joined, and pretty much I have been here every Sunday since the first time I came."

"It was considerate of her to help you through your grief and pain. That is what we as Christians are called to do."

"Yes, I know."

"So you don't always have to be in a church or some formal place for saving to take place, right?" Shaking his head yes hoping she would follow. "Since we are all like Samson, in that God knows us before we are born."

"Yes, I guess so."

"We also know that there was a thief on the cross next to Christ as he hung dying so that our sins could be forgiven who is now in Paradise with Christ. Did you know that?" but without waiting for a response, he continued.

"The thief was dying as surely as our Lord was on that cross. So once he accepted Christ he could do little else, other than die. He could not apologize to the people he had hurt or make any kind of amends. It was too late for that. But even in his dying process he was given an opportunity to begin to know Christ. He took those few moments to do that. Of course, we don't know what happened to Danni. We would all like to know for sure that our loved ones are saved and will be safe throughout eternity. But we don't always get that luxury. You are more blessed than many others. You at least have a record of Danni talking to God, even if she did not know him extremely well. He knew her. And we can both hope that because God knows all of us before we are born, just the way he knew Samson. He knew exactly what was best for Danni even for her unborn child. You have a written record of her talking to God, even praying that Jesus would help her. In an optimal situation, that relationship would have developed and matured over time like yours did. Danni did not have that kind of time. She did, however, like the thief on the cross, have the time to have at least one conversation with Christ. We pray that her prayer was sufficient to save her soul."

"Is that all that you can say, is that we hope the prayer was sufficient?"

"Yes, if I said something other than that, I would be a liar. And you would not want me to lie to you would you?"

"No, I guess not."

"And the truth is Kitera that is all that we can say about everyone because we are all sinners. Every man, woman and child, is a sinner. We all deserve to go to hell, but God has given us the opportunity to avoid hell by accepting Christ as his son and becoming a member of his family. God offers us the opportunity to become his children. I want you to ask yourself this question. Imagine you gave birth to a child but gave that child up for adoption minutes after their birth, and you never saw the child again. Then completely out of the blue one day your doorbell rang, and it was that child. The child looks at you and simply says, I am not sure, but I believe that you may be my mother, and I need your help. Would you welcome that child into your home or would you turn them away?"

"I would probably be happy that the child had found me."

"You are now a follower of Christ. Tell me what you think the Christ that you follow would do in that same situation."

I don't believe that He would turn her away.

I don't either.

"What do you think God, Danni's heavenly Father would do?"

"I hope that he would welcome her in."

We both do. Yet, I am not God. Only God can answer your question for certain. I can't even answer the first question I asked you, 'What would you do?' I don't know for sure what you might take into consideration to make your decision. I can't know for certain what you would do. I can only hope. Can you understand that?"

Yes, she said. It is a little clearer now. Pastor, now that you used the analogy of adoption, I have a question.

Sure what is it?

I remember that, when Thelisa and I first started to read the bible together, we read in Genesis where God said to Noah that people are evil from childhood. He had washed away all of the people and was starting over with just Noah and his family. Why didn't God just make people good, then? He already knew that we would do evil things. After Eve and the snake he knew for certain that we would be disobedient. He knew that we would cause each other a lot of heart aches and Him too probably. Why didn't he do something to stop it in the generations of people that would come after Noah? If he could pluck a rib from Adam and make Eve, it seems that it would have been easy to put something inside of each person to make them obedient. Why does he let us start out evil as if he has given us up for adoption to the world or even to Satan, almost like you said in your example? Why must we find our way back to Him? Why can't we just start out with God, being good and stay that way?

"Deacon Felder was right. You do ask good questions," the Pastor said with a smile and Kitera's serious look lifted, too. I think that passage you are talking about comes from Genesis 8, let's see. Yes, here it is and he read Genesis 8:21. "Never again will I curse the ground because of man, even though every inclination of his heart is evil from childhood."

Yes, that's it.

"Let's see, maybe I can answer your question with a question for you. Is that okay?"

"Sure."

"You've met my wife, Megan right."

Kitera shook her head yes and waited for another question.

"I think that she is beautiful, smart, kind, sassy and fun. She is a loving person, a terrific Mom and so much more. Every morning when I wake up beside her, I am amazed that she is in bed with me. She could have chosen to be with anyone and she could be anywhere in the world. But she is with me. She certainly could have someone with more money, maybe a castle instead of our humble little home, servants, you name it. You get the idea."

Kitera shook her head again in agreement.

"Instead, she has chosen me to love and to be with. Now imagine that she had no choice in the matter. Imagine that we were paired for life without any input into the decision of the person we would be with. Imagine if something in our DNA that we were born with took the entire selection process out of human hands. How much joy would there be in our relationship. How much respect, appreciation or gratitude would we have for each other? I think that much of the joy that I find in believing that she loves me would be lost. If God had decided not to make us in his likeness with the ability to make choices but instead had made us like little tin soldiers, moving at his direction and obeying his orders, how much joy would that bring to him. If we had no options, then having faith would not be part of the equation in our relationship with God. The fact that we can choose, and we do choose Him makes the relationship unique. And more to the point, the fact that He chooses us to love and to receive us as His own is more astonishing to me than my wife choosing me, especially because he knows all of my faults and failures, even the ones I can hide from my wife. Which kind of love would you prefer? Would you want one that is freely given by the person you love or one that is involuntary, coerced? If you could say, I command you to love me and it was done, would you ever be sure that you were really loved? Would you even consider that love?"

No, I suppose not. Pastor, I am glad that I came today to talk with you. I was a little fearful about what would happen, but I am glad that I came.

I am happy that you feel that way, Kitera. Thank you.

The pastor breathed deeply for a second then said, 'Kitera, God is giving you a marvelous opportunity to show the world how grace and mercy should work. I am sorry that I can't tell you what to do with respect to Diondra. You will have to work that out with God for yourself. But I can say that God is always loving towards us. I don't believe that it was by accident that Danni began her relationship with Christ before her death or that she left you a record of that prayer to cherish. I think that it was by God's design because just as we have talked about God knowing Danni, He knows you, as well. God knew the exact thing that you needed to help you get through your daughter's death. So, He lets her talk to you through her writing, send you messages as you call them, even from her grave. I can also say with some certainty that, if you can use this opportunity to help Diondra, you will find that you are being blessed, as well. As Christians, we have a responsibility to forgive others as God has forgiven us. That is not easy because we are, after all, human with many faults and frailties. So, you have done a powerful thing already because you said that you already forgave Diondra for what happened to

Danni. Helping her and her family through this ordeal, although not easy, is probably what Danni would want you to do."

"In fact, I would love to see you, Diondra, Dean and their parents at church together one Sunday if it would not be too painful for you. Maybe one day all of you will feel healed enough and bold enough to tell Danni's story. Maybe Danni's death can be used to prevent some other young person from getting into the same type of trouble."

"That is an excellent idea", Kitera said finally looking a little relived but still undecided about her intentions.

"If you decide to go to court, please let me know, and I will be glad to go with you. If you don't, that is okay too. Just be prayerful about your decision and be guided by the Holy Spirit."

"I will try."

"I hope that this talk helped."

"It did. Anyway, I guess that I will keep reading her diary and try to understand what she and God want me to do." Kitera said sadly. "I will call you to let you know my decision."

"Please do, I will support you either way," Rev. Branford responded trying to sound encouraging.

"Thank you," said Kitera as she rose to shake her pastor's hand.

"You are welcome, Kitera. Remember, you can call on me anytime. I am here for you," he had said remembering his broken promise to Penny.

"May we pray before you leave?"

"Certainly," Kitera's voice trailed off as tears again streamed down her face. "Certainly, she said again as she closed her eyes, imagining Danni in heaven for the first time since her death. Thank you for your notes," she whispered softly. "Thank you."

Chapter 5: Branford's Prayer

Rev. Branford watched from his office window as Kitera Davidson walked through the parking lot, got into her car and began to pull away. Branford's imagination allowed him to envision Kitera as a modern day version of the character Naomi from the book of Ruth in the Bible. In his mind, he compared Naomi's plight with Kitera's because there had been a famine in the country of Bethlehem where Ruth and her family lived. So, they moved to the country of Moab in search of a better life. Similar to Kitera, while living in Moab, Ruth's husband and sons die. Namoi decided to return home. When she arrived in the city, her friends were surprised to see her. They said, 'Can this be Naomi?' Branford imagined that if Kitera's friends saw her now, thin, frail and sad they might ask, "Can this be Kitera?"

Branford could imagine Kitera thinking, much like Naomi did that God had been unkind to her. He was glad, however, that like Naomi, who heard that God was providing food for the people in Bethlehem and decided to go home; Kitera had heard the God was feeding people food for their souls at Hope and Grace. Kitera's famine had been a spiritual one. He hoped that God would be as generous to Kitera as he had been to Naomi because eventually, God blessed Naomi in more ways than she could have ever expected. Branford prayed that God would bless Kitera also, and he prayed that God would use him to feed her His Word.

He lingered at the window for a little while after her car was out of sight, then sat down at his desk and began to make notes about their meeting. After writing a brief summary, he searched his bookshelf and began removing books on grief counseling that he thought would be helpful to review as he critiqued of himself and his counseling session with Kitera. Had his words been comforting he wondered. 'Did I lead her in the right direction,' he asked himself as he grabbed a book on forgiveness and began reading it. Branford would read far into the night. He was concerned about how he had handled his session with Kitera. How, he wondered, would she arrive at a decision about how to handle Diondra's mother's request to help save her daughter from going to jail. And as he thought about Diondra's parents his heart filled with sorrow. He could not imagine the pain they must be in as they waited for Kitera's answer to their request to help their daughter. 'Will she plead with the judge for leniency for Diondra?' he wondered. Even if she does decide to help, will the judge take her request into consideration as he made his decision? This situation is heartbreaking for everyone involved, he concluded.

Then, he posed the question 'Could I be that forgiving if it were my child?' to himself. But he could not give an honest, definitive answer to the question. Not even in the privacy of his own office; with no one but himself and God present could he answer the question. He could only hope that he would do what was right.

Before closing the last book, he prayed again for Kitera Davidson. This time he included Diondra, Dean, and their parents, Carla and Andrew in his prayer. He recited Deuteronomy 6:5:7:

Love the LORD your God with all your heart and with all your soul and with all your strength. These commandments that I give you today are to be on your hearts. Impress them on your children. Talk about them when you sit at home and when you walk along the road, when you lie down and when you get up.

He prayed for all of the parents of the children that would needlessly be lost to the grave or to jail in the days to come. He prayed for the lost children already languishing in prisons, and he prayed for parents that would only think about their child's soul after the casket was closed for the last time. He prayed for parents who were trying hard to teach their children about God. Sadness filled him as he prayed for children everywhere; especially those children who would become parents while still children themselves. He prayed that all children would have an opportunity to get to know Christ.

Branford, with salty tears streaming down his face, pleaded with God, to protect his own family. "Keep my children safe," he begged remembering the look on Kitera's face as she announced that her daughter was dead. "Keep them free of all hurt, harm and danger. Lord, I spend so much time away from them. Be with them in my absence. Help me to fulfill my responsibilities to my family even as I nurture the members of Hope and Grace. As I listen to your children's pains, help them work through their hurts and answer their questions, guide my tongue, let me keep their secrets safely locked in my heart. "Lord help me to be the father to my own children, husband to my wife and pastor to your children that you want me to be. Amen."

Branford stood up, looked at the mess on his desk, and decided to put off cleaning it up until the next morning. It had been a long day, and he was ready for his bed. "Tomorrow, I'll start anew," he thought as he took his coat from the closet. "I need to go and sneak a hug from my kids."

Chapter 6: Kitera's Decision

Clarissa knocked then opened the door to the pastor's office, but Rev. Branford did not notice her. He was too deep in thought about Kitera to be aware of Clarissa's presence.

"Pastor, you have not been yourself for the past few days. Is everything alright? What's the problem?"

"Oh, no, problem," Branford replied.

"Well you are sure acting like there is. You seem distracted and distant, are you sure everything is okay?"

"Yes, I'm sure. Thank you for asking. What's up?" Branford asked as he tried to put a smile on his face.

"Ms. Kitera Davidson is in my office. She would like to see you; if that's okay. She doesn't have an appointment, so if you rather that she comes back at another time, I will make an appointment for her."

"No, she is that's great! Please send her in," Branford said with more enthusiasm than Clarissa had heard in the Pastor's voice all week.

"Okay, I will send her right in," Clarissa said as she turned and left the room.

A few moments later, Kitera Davidson walked into the Pastor's office. Clarissa trailed her, and once she was inside closed the door behind Kitera without saying anything.

"Hello, Kitera. Come in please and have a seat," Branford said as he rose from his chair.

"Thank you for seeing me on such short notice," Kitera said as she sat down in front of the pastor's desk.

"How have you been?" Branford asked.

"I've been well," she said responding to Branford's question. "Just prayerfully trying to make a decision about what to do about Diondra's hearing, like you said I should," Kitera answered.

"So, have you come to a decision?" Branford asked.

"Yes," she responded.

Fishing for a longer response Branford asked, "Did you decide to make a statement at Diondra's hearing?"

"No," she said.

"I see," Branford said as he felt his heart sink.

Noticing the pastor's crestfallen face Kitera hurriedly said, "I mean, yes I am going to attend the hearing, but I am going to let someone else be the character witness for Diondra?"

"Oh, I see," Branford said, a little relieved. "Who will it be your mother?" Branford guessed; remembering their conversation about how her mother had helped her when her daughter, Danni died.

"No, Danni," she said.

"Danni," the pastor said raising his eyebrows.

"Yes, you see Diondra could not have a better character witness than Danni," she said smiling.

"But, how will that be possible," Branford questioned her.

"I am going to use Danni's own words, the words in her diaries, to show the judge what kind of person Diondra is and the relationship that she had with Danni. Anyone hearing what Danni has to say about Diondra would know that what happen was an accident. There is no way that Diondra would have intentionally hurt Danni," Kitera said with confidence.

Remembering the portion of Danni's diary that Kitera had read to him during their first meeting, he could see why she would believe that Danni's own words would be persuasive.

"I am going to read a message that Danni wrote about getting her glasses. Kitera began telling the pastor the story: "When Danni was nine we noticed that she was having trouble with her vision; so I took her for an eye exam. The doctor said that she needed eyeglasses and that she would need to wear them at all times; unless she was sleeping. Danni was extremely upset because she thought that the kids at school would tease her. She was sure that her classmates would call her four eyes. She gave me a hard time about needing the glasses during the days before we actually picked them up. She tried to convince me that she could see perfectly well without them but to no avail of course. On the first day that she was supposed to wear the glasses to school she would not even put them on before we left the house"

"Kids can be like that," Branford injected.

"Yes, but as soon as she got to school, Diondra asked her where her eyeglasses were."

"Danni wrote, 'Diondra made me put on my eyeglasses and when I did she told me that I looked smart! Diondra said that I was like the scarecrow in the "Wizard of Oz" all I needed were the glasses to make me look intelligent.' She drew smiley faces wearing glasses under the paragraph. On the next page she wrote, "Di called over all of our friends to where we were standing and said to them, 'Doesn't Danni look smarter with her glasses on, like a real professor.' They all agreed that I did she said, and congratulated me instead of teasing me. It was a great day. Di is the best friend ever!"

"It seems that they were such good friends. It really is a shame what happened," Branford lamented.

"Yes, and then there was the evening that Danni got her first period. She called Diondra first thing, and of course, Diondra insisted that her father drive her over to our house immediately. She wanted to bring Danni something special to celebrate. When Diondra got there, she made Danni a cup of hot tea with her special ingredient. Danni loved it. Diondra convinced Danni that they should sit at the kitchen table, drink their tea and discuss life. Diondra said 'since we are both "women" now we should have tea.' Danni wrote that they could not find much to discuss, so they decided to play the card game, "Old Maid" instead. 'Di always knows how to make me feel better,' Danni wrote."

"What was Diondra's special ingredient?" Branford asked, curious to know.

"Peppermint candy and Danni loved it."

"Cute."

"There are so many more stories in Danni's diary like those two. Another one that I am going to read if the judge will allow it is from the time that Danni got her braces, Diondra stayed over all week-end making her Jell-O and chocolate ice cream shakes. "I just love Di," Danni wrote.

"Now, I understand why you believe that Danni will be Diondra's best character witness."

"Do you truly believe that I am right to do it this way?"

"Yes, and I hope that the judge is persuaded not only by Danni's words but by your forgiveness of Diondra. I hope that you will let the judge know that you have forgiven Diondra and that you do not want her punished any further."

"Yes, I will. If the judge listens and lets her go free that will be a blessing beyond measure. I have been praying that we will all walk out of the court free and together, Diondra, Dean, Carla, Andrew and me. Not just free of the charges and sentencing but free of the pain and the hurt that all of this has caused. I know that my heart will always ache for Danni. But I also know that nothing good can come out of Diondra going to jail. That is not what Danni would want to happen. I believe in my heart that what happened was an accident and that Diondra would do anything to have those few seconds when she pushed Danni back. But life does not work that way. Sometimes, we don't get do overs. So, we must move on and live the life that God has given to us."

"Kitera, you cannot imagine how glad I am to hear you say that. I have been praying for you and the Davis family constantly since we had our last meeting. I am sure that God will work everything out for everyone's benefit."

"Thank you, Pastor; I have faith that God will do just that, too."

They both sat quietly thinking for a moment.

"Pastor," Kitera said interrupting the silence. "When I spoke to Carla to let her know that I would be at the hearing and what I planned to do, I also told her about you. I told her how much you had helped me to make my decision about this situation. I asked Carla if she had any objection to you coming to the hearing."

"I hope that she said that she did not."

"She did, and Pastor, Carla also wants to know if you would meet with us, her family and me before the hearing. She wondered if you would pray with us before the hearing. If you are there with us, I know I will feel much better about everything, too."

"Great, I would love to be there for all of you. It would be my honor to do that," Branford said as he thought to himself. "God does answer prayers."

"The hearing is next Monday at 9:00 a.m.; can you meet us at 8:15 a.m. in the courthouse lobby?" Kitera asked.

"Sure, thank you so much for asking me," Branford said.

"No, I thank you and most of all I thank God for helping me to get through this," Kitera said.

Branford could only smile at Kitera's statement before asking, "Is there anything else."

"No, not a thing. Why, don't you think that is enough," Kitera joked for the first time in a long time.

"It is more than enough," Branford teased back, "More than enough," he repeated.

"It is good to see you smile."

"Thank you. Now that I believe that there will be a good resolution to this situation, I feel like I have something to smile about," Kitera confessed.

"Great. I am happy for you. Are you ready?" Branford asked.

"Yes," Kitera answered.

"Then let's pray."

Say It Ain't So

Prelude: Am I a Sinner?

When Rev. Joshua Branford opened the large shopping bag with the tee shirts for his family from the Evangelism Team and read the new outreach slogan printed on them, *"Grateful Sinner Saved By Grace,"* his youngest daughter, Penny immediately asked, "Am I a sinner, Daddy?"

Before he could answer her question, his son, Jai jumped in. "Are you a sinner? Are you kidding me? Of course, you are a sinner. A biggggg one," he exaggerated the word. "As much trouble as you are always getting into how could you not be one."

"But Daddy," Penny pleaded, "Sinners go to the bad place when they die. I don't want to go there."

Jai held up two fingers behind Penny's head to look like horns. Penny pushed his arm away.

"Jai cut it out.

"But Dad, I was only kidding."

"You heard me," Joshua said to Jai. Then Joshua asked, "Penny do you know what hopeful means?"

"Yes. It means that you are hoping for something. Like I'm hoping for some more ice cream right now," Penny said cleverly working her request for more dessert into the conversation.

"Yes, well, I don't know about the ice cream part, you will have to ask Mommy if you can have more ice cream. But that is exactly what hopeful means. It means that you are looking forward to something. You are expecting something to happen."

"Okay." she said smiling because she got it right.

"And, yes, we believe that every person is a sinner.

"Everybody?" Penny's eyebrows rose showing her surprise at his answer.

"Yes," he confirmed.

"Even you, Daddy? And Mommy?" Penny asked incredulously.

"Yes, even me and Mommy," he confirmed. "That is why the words *grateful sinner* is on each tee shirt. Grateful is an important word in the sentence because although the members of Hope and Grace are sinners, we are very grateful to God for sending His son who died and then rose from the dead so that we could go to heaven. Just like you should be grateful that Mommy is getting you more ice cream, although you probably don't deserve it.

Why, did you say that, Daddy?

Did you eat all of your dinner?

"No, I had to save room for my desert."

"How about room for more peas?"

"Noooo, just ice cream, Daddy."

That's why I said that you don't deserve it. You did not do what you were supposed to, which was to eat all of your dinner before dessert. Right? But your mother loves you and so she is giving you dessert that you don't deserve, instead of the peas that you do deserve." he continued his explanation. "We are grateful because God he loved us so much that he sent his son Jesus Christ to save us from going to hell, the bad place, which is what we deserve. Instead we get to live with God in heaven."

"Oh, so I'm a sinner, but I am not going to the bad place, right Daddy."

"Right, because you are saved by God's grace." Branford wanted to continue the conversation and to explain more about being saved, not just for Penny's benefit but for Abigail's and Jai's as well, but Penny interrupted him.

"This is so yummy. Mommy thank you for the ice cream. See I'm grateful Daddy." Penny said as she shoveled another spoonful of ice cream in her mouth, and then asked the burning question on her mind, "Mommy, can I have sprinkles on top this time." She was more interested at that moment in her stomach than her soul. And just like that their conversation was over.

"Another time," Joshua thought as he sat down to dinner with his family. After questioning his own motives, for a second, for not capitalizing on the moment, he frowned and wondered how many parents had said 'another time' without knowing that there would not be 'another time.' Even after recognizing his failure he did not attempt to reopen the conversation. Instead, he mouthed the words to his wife, "Sorry for being late but she did not respond."

Tomorrow, Rev. Branford would need to remind himself more than once that every person is a sinner including himself. He would also be reminded that there are no big sins, no little sins, just sins. He would also learn that the age of a person is not a determining factor in the magnitude of devastation that dishonesties can cause.

Chapter 1: Cheaters Never Win

Pulling onto the black asphalt church parking lot, and turning into the white-lined space, with the rectangle shaped sign in front of it that read, Reserved for the Pastor, Rev. Branford could see Clarissa, his secretary, through the church office window. He smiled as the song, "Baby Got Back" popped into his head while he watched her bend down to put paper into the copy machine's paper tray. Looking up as if praying then chuckling he said, "Lord, thank you for taking me out of the streets but you've got a long way to go to take the streets out of me." Branford laughed even harder to himself.

"This is not the way to get ready for my day," he said under his breath. "Lord, help me to behave," he jokingly prayed and then laughed out loud.

Branford parked the car, got out and opened the back car door to get his briefcase when he noticed the scuffed purple and white book bag lying on the floor. "Oh, no." he grumbled aloud. The bag had his daughter Penny's ballet gear in it.

"Man, I was supposed to leave that bag with Mom when I dropped Penny off this morning. I'm in trouble," he thought slamming the car door shut and leaving the purple bag lying on the floor of the car.

The Reverend imagined seeing his six-year-old daughter's "I told you so" face as he replayed their morning's conversation in his head. "Daddy, remember Mommy said don't forget my ballet stuff. It's in my purple book bag. She is going to take me straight to my lesson when she picks me up," she had announced gleefully.

"I've got it, Pen," he half snarled at her as he grabbed the bag from the kitchen counter. Rev. Branford was convinced that six year old Penny had decided that it was her job to remind him of all of the "honey-do" things on his wife's daily list of chores for him. Funny, he thought, how Penny could never remember her own list, but his she always remembered perfectly.

Penny had looked up at him from fastening her jacket just in time to see him snatch up the bag. He noticed her smile and said, "I see that smirk, smarty pants."

"What would you do without me, Daddy," she laughed.

"Well, let me see," he replied.

"Don't even try it, Daddy, you wouldn't know what to do without me," she said so confidently that he had to laugh.

"Is that so?" he said.

"Yes," she said in her emphatic I-am-going-to-be-a-woman-someday voice.

"If you say so," he said as they made their way down the hall towards the front door.

"Race you to the car, Daddy," Penny said just before he opened the door. "Last one is a rotten egg," she yelled knowing that he needed to lock the door before he could take off in their race to the car.

Instead of locking the door he surprised her by swooping her up and running with her and her bag in his arms to the car touching it first.

"No fair," Penny said with a pout.

"Why, because I didn't let you cheat me?"

She gave him her Cheshire cat grin and said, "I know, cheaters never win."

"You are right." He told her. Then he opened the back door to the car and tossed the purple bag in on the seat next to her car seat.

"Climb in while I go back and lock the door, okay baby. Fasten your seat belt, too."

"Okay, but next time I am going to win, Daddy," she said still pouting. "Just wait and see."

He could not help but wonder if the bag had fallen off the seat by accident or if his adorable little Penny had pushed it off of the seat on purpose. Either way he would have to get the bag to her before time for her ballet practice or he was sure he would not hear the end of it, from Penny or her Mom.

"Good morning Clarissa, how was your weekend?" Rev. Branford asked in a loud but melodic voice as he strode down the hall leading to his office.

"Fine, Pastor and yours," she answered back.

"It was great," he responded.

Standing at the door of Clarissa's office, he said, "I saw you at the early morning service yesterday. It is growing nicely, don't you think?"

"Yes, I thought that I would come and check it out."

"Speaking of checking things out, you better watch how you bend over in front of that window, or I might have to become a Catholic just so I can go to confession," he teased.

"Pastor, you know you ought to quit it," she called back to him as he placed his key into his office door.

"No, you are the one who ought to quit it," he continued their playful exchange. "But it is all good. You just make me have to pray that much harder."

"Yeah, and you make me have to pray for you that much harder, too," Clarissa, laughed.

"So what's on the schedule for today?" he said in a more serious voice as he hung his jacket in the small closet in his office.

"Well, you have a meeting this morning with Minister Gabrian at 10:00AM to go over the new Bible study classes and you have a noon meeting with Samantha Leigh. She said that she had a few early appointments but that she should be here by 12:15.

After that, you are free until your three thirty appointment." She finished her reply by reminding him that there was a copy of his schedule for the week on his desk.

"I know, Mizz. EEEEfficient, I was just trying to help keep you on your toes," he quipped. "Clarissa, see if you can get Molly Frye on the phone, please. I need to find out how her father is doing. Molly told me yesterday that her father is in the hospital. I promised to try to get by to see him. Get his first name again, and ask her, which hospital he is in. Please, let her know that I will see him no later than tomorrow. Maybe I can visit with him this afternoon if my meeting with Samantha doesn't last too long. Do you have any idea what Samantha wants?

"No, the phone was ringing this morning when I walked in the office. I answered it and it was Samantha. She asked me to set-up an appointment for her with you for as soon as possible. So, after checking your schedule, I told her that she could come in today at noon. I did ask her what the meeting was in reference to; she said that it was a personal matter that she needed to discuss with you. I left it at that," Clarissa said as she pulled the new member, Molly Frye's information up on her computer screen and began dialing her phone number.

"Hello," a sleepy voice answered the phone.

"May I speak to Molly Frye," Clarissa said.

"This is she," Molly answered trying to rouse herself from her deep sleep. "I hope this is not a sales call," she thought to herself. She usually turned the phone off before going to sleep after working a double shift at the hospital, but today she left it on just in case she got a call from the doctor about her Dad.

"Hi, Molly, I'm sorry did I wake you? This is Clarissa, Rev. Branford's secretary. He asked me to give you a call to find out which hospital your Dad is in. He is going to try and get by to see him today."

"Oh, thank you so much," Molly said, happy that her pastor was going to visit her Dad, even after she told him her Dad was a non-believer.

"How is your Dad?" Clarissa asked as Molly looked at the pad on her nightstand for the phone number to her father's room.

"He is coming along. We are waiting for some test results so the doctors can tell how much damage was done to his heart muscle during the heart attack." Molly replied then gave Clarissa the information she had requested.

"I hope that everything works out alright," Clarissa said as she typed the last of the information Molly had given her and sent the message to the pastor's phone.

"Keep us in your prayers, and thank the pastor for me," Molly said before hanging up the receiver.

"I will. God bless," Clarissa said as she placed the receiver back in its cradle and began imputing the information on Molly's father, Benjamin Frye in Molly's membership folder.

Chapter 2: Samantha

The creaky door to the Pastor's office opened and in stepped a smiling Samantha Leigh. "Thank you for seeing me on such short notice," Samantha Leigh said as she hurried into the pastor's study after Clarissa announced her on the intercom. She closed the door and made sure it was secure before heading toward the cushiony rust colored leather chair stationed in front of the pastor's desk. Samantha was dressed in a silk periwinkle blouse and gray tweed skirt that showed off her long coco brown legs. Her gray suede pumps matched the stylish suede clutch handbag she carried. She wore a gold necklace, which held a cross on it that she fiddled nervously with as she made her way across the room.

"No problem Samantha, please have a seat," the pastor said rising slightly from his seat behind his desk. When she seemed comfortable in her seat, he sat back down and said, "It is good to see you. I enjoyed the solo you did with the choir yesterday. It was very moving."

"Thank you. I like singing with the choir, although doing solos are not exactly my forte."

"You could have fooled me. You did a great job. In fact, I hope to hear you more often." In a more measured voice, he inquired, "So what's on your mind Samantha, how can I help you?"

Samantha took a deep breath and began, "First off, I don't know if you are aware that my husband is incarcerated."

"No, I didn't know, and I am sorry to hear that. Was he arrested recently?"

"No, in fact, he is about to get out of prison, which is why I am here."

"Really, do you mind telling me why he was sent to jail?"

"No, he shot a man," Samantha said tersely.

"Was he a member of a gang?"

Oh, no, nothing like that. He was trying to protect his sister Cassie and her girls from her crazy husband, Evron. For all of the good that it did."

"And his sister's relationship with her husband got so bad that your husband felt that he had to shoot him. Why? What happened?"

"Well, his sister Cassie was a screw-up then and still is now. But to hear her tell it; they are both victims of my husband, Samuel. It was like this, Cassie and her husband Evron were both drug users, which is bad enough by itself, but Evron was also very abusive both verbally and physically to Cassie and their kids. And it's a shame too because, they have two girls and they are as sweet as can be."

"I see," Branford said, nodding to encourage her to continue.

"It really all amounted to Samuel being fed up with the situation and taking matters into his own hands, and in the process making matters worse for everyone, especially himself."

"Yes, trying to fix other people's lives seldom turns out the way we plan."

"I know, and I tried to tell him that. You see, a week before Samuel shot Evron; Evron had beaten Cassie pretty badly. He broke several of her ribs, and her nose. And he did it right in front of his girls. When Samuel found out he swore that if he saw Evron again he would hurt him."

"I can understand his feeling that way." Branford said to Samantha's surprise.

"When we got to the hospital the police were with Cassie and the girls. The girls were so distraught; you cannot imagine what that was like for them. We helped to convince Cassie that night that she should file charges against Evron and that they both needed to get some help with their drug problems. We all thought that if Evron were in jail, he would be out of everybody's hair, at least for a while. That would have given everybody a chance to calm down."

"So, was he arrested?" Branford asked.

"Yes, Cassie pressed charges while she was at the hospital and the police arrested him at their home. Samuel and I helped her to get into a shelter for battered women. We had high hopes that things would get better for her and her girls."

"What went wrong?" Branford said.

"Evron's mother got him out on bail. That is what went wrong."

"How long was he in prison?"

"Over night," Samantha said.

The pastor raised his eyebrows at her answer.

"Yes, you got it. The very next day Evron went home and found that Cassie and the girls were not there.

His first night out he was harassing Samuel's mother with phone calls trying to find out where Cassie was. Then the next day high on something Evron went to Samuel's mother's house looking for Cassie with a gun. He threatened to shoot her if she did not tell him where Cassie was. When she would not tell him, he started breaking up things, plates from the china cabinet and a window in the dining room trying to convince her to tell him. When that did not work, he told her that he was going to the school to see his girls. He stormed out swearing he'd come back and kill her if he did not find them." She said in a strained voice.

"Your mother-in-law was fortunate that he did not hurt her, but she must have been horrified all the same. Did she call the police?"

"No, she did not," Samantha said angrily. "As soon as Evron left her house, my mother-in-law called Samuel instead of calling the police. She was upset and screaming that Evron was going to kill the girls.

When Samuel got off the phone, he didn't call the police either. He was so angry. It was like he was out of his mind with rage."

"I can imagine that your mother-in-law was not thinking clearly after having her life threatened that way and that your husband felt that he had to do something - albeit he made a wrong choice, by not calling the police - but I can understand wanting to do something drastic," Rev. Branford said.

"I know. That is why I sometimes blame my mother-in-law for this entire situation. She had to know that Samuel would go after Evron once she told him that he had threatened her with the gun, especially after all that had happened the previous week."

"Had Samuel and Evron ever been violent with each other before?"

"No, they had never come to blows before. But Samuel had been on the verge for a while. He just kept praying and hoping that his sister would turn her life around, come to her senses and leave Evron. Nothing we could say to her had ever seemed to penetrate. Which is why we were all so happy, my mother-in-law, Samuel and I when she went to the shelter? We were hoping that it was finally over between them. Personally, I think that when Evron showed up and threatened my mother-in-law that she genuinely wanted him dead. I don't think that she'd ever admit it, but I think that his mother actually wanted Samuel to find Evron and kill him. She was tired of living with the fear of what might happen to her daughter and her grand kids. We all were. We were all tired of waiting for the knock on the door or the phone call letting us know that Cassie and the kids were hurt or dead. His mom was scared, angry and as weary as we were of Evron abusing Cassie. Plus, on that day, I know that she thought as insane as Evron was he might really make good on his threat and hurt the girls when he got to the school if he could not find Cassie. Anyway she called Samuel and that call set everything else in motion. I don't know. Sometimes I think I shouldn't be so hard on her. We have not had a very close relationship since all of this happened. I blamed her for Samuel going to jail. I think she blames herself, too. But Samuel says that it was his fault. His alone. He knew better."

"How did Samuel end up shooting Evron? What led to him actually doing something that drastic?"

"We all thought that Evron might one day kill Cassie and the girls if nothing changed. That was one of the reasons we purposely did not bring the girls to our house or to my mother-in-law's home when Cassie got out of the hospital. We wanted to keep Evron from finding her and trying to influence her to come back to him. After Cassie finally agreed to go to the shelter and get a restraining order against Evron to keep him away from her and the girls, I thought that things were going to work themselves out okay. Cassie had even agreed to go get treatment for her addiction. We were just waiting for a bed to become available so that she could be admitted. We thought that we could finally breathe a little easier and that we were finally going to be rid of Evron. But Evron could not leave well enough alone. After Evron showed up at Samuel's mother's house waving a gun like a madman, and threatening to kill everybody in the family if Cassie did not come back to him, Samuel's mother then made that hysterical call to Samuel at the high school where he was teaching."

"Your husband is a teacher?"

"Yes. He was a teacher until his mother got him all worked up about finding and stopping Evron before he could hurt somebody. That call sent Samuel flying off half-cocked. He went to our house and got a pistol that had belonged to his father. His mother had given it to him after his father died, and he kept it hidden and locked up in the attic. Knowing that Evron was not going to find the girls at school because they were not there, Samuel figured that he would give up sooner or later and want to buy more drugs. So he drove around to some of Evron's drug haunts, waited a couple of hours and sure enough, Evron showed up. Samuel just got out of his car didn't say a word to Evron. He walked up to Evron aimed and shot him before he knew what was even going on. Thank God that he did not kill him."

"That's good."

"But Evron did end up paralyzed and will be in a wheelchair for the rest of his life."

"That's tough."

Looking as though she was about to cry Samantha continued, "Pastor, my husband is a good man. He was a teacher at the high school, and he coached the football team. Everybody loved and respected him. Now he has ruined his life and ours, in a sense, over nothing. I don't know what is going to happen now when he is released. I don't know what kind of job he will be able to get; certainly, he will not be able to go back to work as a teacher. Worst of all, it makes me nuts because this whole thing did not have to happen. Samuel wanted to go after Evron when he saw Cassie at the hospital like I said, but I was able to calm him down then. I told him to let the police handle it. Just let the police handle it, that is what they are paid for, but this time no one was there to talk him down. To top it all off, Cassie is back with her fool husband Evron. After the shooting, she stayed with him at the hospital. She didn't even call to ask how Samuel was doing after he was locked up.

"Really,"

"Yes, really. Now, she takes care of Evron like he is some kind of king, even though her mother says he is still nasty to her. He tells her that she owes it to him to take care of him, and he treats her like dirt. She is still making all kinds of excuses for him. She apparently believes that he is entitled to treat her like a slave because it was her brother that paralyzed him. It's crazy. Meanwhile, Evron does not take any responsibility for anything that has happened to him. In my opinion, Cassie and Evron are both still out of their minds. But at least they are not on drugs. I guess if there is one good thing that came out of this is that their girls have a better life because their parents are not doing drugs." She stopped and took a deep breath looking drained from the retelling of her story.

She started again, "Don't misunderstand me Pastor, Samuel is a kind, smart and loving man," she emphasized the word loving as she cupped her chin in her hand. "The kind of man any women would want to marry. Under ordinary circumstances, he would not hurt a fly, but when it comes to protecting his mother and sisters, he becomes a completely different animal. He has been trying to take care of them since he was twelve. That was how old he was when his father died," shaking her head she said resolutely, "but that is a whole other story," she stopped herself in what almost seemed like mid-thought. "Anyway, I did not mean to rehash that old story, let me get to what brings me here today."

"Are you sure that you don't want to discuss some of the issues you just talked about. Although they happened some time ago you seem to be having some trouble dealing with them even now."

"I know, but what I need to talk to you about today is my most pressing issue right now."

"Alright then," Branford said exhaling as he asked himself, "What could possibly be more troubling than the story she told me?"

"Okay, this is my problem," Samantha said pragmatically as she began her story again. "Samuel is about to be released from jail and believe me, I will be extremely glad that he will be home. None of what has happened has changed my love for him. I want you to understand that, but I uh, I" and she stopped short of stating the problem.

"Yes," Rev. Branford prodded.

"Well, you see, I, I, I'm afraid that Samuel might be sick," she blurted out quickly.

"Sick?" Branford repeated slowly furling his brow.

"Yes, I'm afraid that he might be infected with HIV, and I am not sure what I should do."

"Is there some specific reason why you believe he might be infected? Has Samuel been ill?"

"No nothing as concrete as that. In fact, I had not actually given it any thought until about three weeks ago when Larine invited me to the luncheon given by the Prison Ministry. There was a speaker there, and she talked about the high number of men in the prison systems that are infected with HIV. She talked about how much greater the HIV infection rate is for men and women inside prison than for people who are not incarcerated. It didn't truly hit me at first because I know that my husband is straight. Then she started to talk about the high number of rapes that take place in jail. That started me thinking. By the time she said that some men don't even consider themselves homosexual if they have sex with another man while locked up, I was scared. I know that Samuel would not do anything like that willingly but I don't know what has gone on while he has been away. I do know that he got into a fight and was in solitary for a short time, but he did not want to talk about it when I asked him what happened. Slowing her speech down just a little," Samantha asked, "Pastor, do you think that I am overreacting?"

"No, not at all. Have you talked to Samuel about your concerns?"

"I tried to. I told him about the luncheon and started telling him what they said about the HIV epidemic and the prison statistics." He interrupted me and said, "Yeah, yeah I know can we talk about something else please?" I wanted Samuel to know that I was worried about him. He got mad. Then he had the nerve to ask me if I was trying to insinuate that he was gay or something. I told him no, it was not about him being gay or anything like that. After that, I just dropped the subject. Now, that I know for sure that he is about to come home, I don't know what to do. I believe that I need to know for sure before we do anything, you understand what I mean?"

"Sure, I think that you have a legitimate reason for concern, and you need to think about Junior, yourself, as well as Samuel. You have a right to know that it is safe to resume your normal marital relationship with him. The crime of rape is degrading and hideous, so I understand how your questioning your husband about that might be an affront to his manhood, but I agree with you that you need and have a right to know. It seems to me that you are saying that you don't want him to be tested because you are blaming him for anything, but to allay the bona-fide fear that you have about him possibly being sick. Also, so you can make whatever adjustments in your lifestyle that might be necessary if he is positive. Is that correct?"

"Yes, that is exactly the reason I want him to be tested when he gets out. Not so, I can blame him or leave him, I just want to make an informed, educated decision about my life, about our lives."

"Yes, and Samuel himself should want to know that it is safe for you to be with him without using some kind of precaution, right? Because he loves you and wants you to be safe and well."

"Yes, yes," she nodded her head in agreement.

"Then why don't you suggest to Samuel that you both get tested?"

"Both?" she said in a raised voice interrupting the pastor's response. "Why in the world would I need to be tested? I love Samuel, and I have been faithful to him. There is no reason that I should get tested."

The pastor could feel Samantha's outrage with him, but he continued. "I will bet that Samuel felt the same way that you just did when I suggested to you that you get tested, when you talked to him about getting tested. He may have felt that you were questioning his love for you, but you were not, right?"

"Yes," she said more quietly.

"I would suggest that you let Samuel know that you know that he loves you. Let him know that being tested has nothing to do with love. You have both been away from each other for some time, and while neither of you is accusing the other of allowing certain things to happen, you just want to reassure and to be sure that everything is what it should be. You are not questioning his love, loyalty or manhood; you just want to start afresh with his mind at ease and yours as well that everything is all right. Likewise, you know that he is not questioning your fidelity or love, but you have to admit that you have had as much opportunity as he had to be with other people while he was away - maybe even more. So,

170

you should want to put his mind at ease, as well. You are a very attractive, intelligent," he said smiling at the woman "and things could have happened with you as well as with him. After all, he did not leave you with a locked chastity belt on while he was away. Perhaps, if you suggest that you both be tested it will make it an easier pill to swallow for Samuel."

"Maybe, I had not thought of it that way. I will think about it. I don't want to put any crazy ideas in his head either."

"Believe me neither of you is crazy to want to be safe."

"When is he being released?"

"Junior and I are picking him up on Wednesday. Junior got his driver's license while his dad was away, and he can't wait to take him for a spin."

"Will you talk to Samuel before you pick him up?"

"Yes, we talk often, so I am sure that I will talk to him before we pick him up?"

"Great then why don't you try talking to him again about being tested over the phone, giving him some time to think about it before he comes home? I read somewhere recently that there is a rapid test that will give you the results in about twenty minutes. Maybe your family doctor can do it for you. You should take the test as soon as possible. This way both of you will be able to put this behind you and celebrate his homecoming; however, you like."

"That sounds like a plan. I will tell you how everything turns out." Samantha said as she stood up.

"Great. And Samantha if you or anyone in your family wants to talk about what has happened or what is happening just give me a call. Let's pray before you leave."

Chapter 3: Prom Princess

Clarissa pushed the button for the Rev. Branford's private line on the phone and announced, "Pastor, your three thirty is here.

"Thank you," Branford replied.

"Oh, yeah" she continued, "I took Penny's book bag to your Mother's house while I was out for lunch

"Thanks."

"And before I forget, Penny said to tell you, 'hello'. She also said that she knew you would forget her bag." Clarissa's lilted teasing voice streamed through the intercom.

"Send Zarina in please and thank you very much," not amused at all by Clarissa's last statement. Rev.

Branford quickly scanned his notes from the previous week in Zarina's folder. He had hoped that Penny was taking her nap when Clarissa dropped off the bag that way she would never find out that he had forgotten to leave the bag that morning after she reminded him about it. "Ah, well, no such luck."

He looked up as his young congregant gingerly opened the door and sashayed into the office all ready to tell him her rehearsed story about the prom dress her grandparents purchased for her. The last thing that Zarina wanted to do was sit down with the Pastor again to talk about her "problem". But because her grandmother insisted she thought it best to try to make him think she was just a happy go-lucky kid. "Everybody likes you better when your most difficult problem is picking out a prom dress," she thought, just before she pasted a smile on her face and opened the pastor's door.

"Hello," rising slightly from his seat, Rev. Branford welcomed the youngster into the office.

Zarina was sixteen, but could easily pass for twelve in her plaid blue and yellow button down shirt and blue jeans. She wore flat navy blue shoes with a gold buckles on the toes that made her appear even shorter than her five-two frame. Her black hair was neatly braided and hung loosely down around her wispy shoulders. Zarina's face had a fresh glowing look about it, and Rev. Branford noted that she was not wearing make-up like some of the teenage girls in his congregation. She flashed him a broad smile as she entered the office but as hard as she tried there was an underlying sadness in her eyes that her smile could not mask. Branford directed her to the seat nearest him. "She is so young for this discussion he thought to himself."

"How are you, Zarina?"

"I'm fine, how are you Pastor?" Zarina, reaching to shake the pastor's hand, said before taking her seat.

"I am okay," he replied feigning a quick smile. "So tell me, how has your week been?"

"Oh, things are going great. I finally found the perfect dress for the prom." Reaching over pictures of the pastor's family on the oversized wooden glass covered desk, she held up the dog-eared picture of a fresh-faced teenage model wearing a long lavender silk taffeta dress with a strapless sweetheart neckline that Zarina had cut from a magazine. "My grandmother is going to add a few pearls at the neckline and the waist," she said as she gestured to the picture. "She is going do few other alterations, too so that it fits me like a glove," she continued. "It is going to be great. We are going to pick out shoes on Saturday. Granny said that I can even get the shoes dyed to match the dress if I want, too."

"You sound much cheerier today than you did last week. Are things going better between you and your grandmother?"

"Well, kinda," she said hesitantly, wanting to stay focused on the prom and the lighter things in her life.

"What does kinda mean?"

"I don't know. I just try to tell her what she wants to hear mostly. That makes it better for everybody."

"Does that mean that you are not being honest with her?"

"Well, I figured that the reason she is worried about me is because she is in my business too much. So I stopped telling her certain things."

"You stopped telling her things like what?" Branford asked.

"Mostly, I stopped telling her where I am going. She doesn't worry if I tell her things like; I am going to the library. So, that is what I tell her."

"Are you saying that you tell her that you are going to the library when you are actually going someplace else?"

"Sometimes. I mean I am just trying to have a normal life. I don't know why that is so hard for everybody to understand. When my parents decided that I should move here with my grandparents everyone said that it was so I could have a normal life, now my grandmother keeps trying to mess that up. It's not fair!" trying to mentally crawl back into her happy face Zarina stopped talking and just stared wide-eyed at the pastor.

"What does normal mean to you, Zarina?"

"Just that. It means doing normal stuff. Normal, that's all."

"Okay, then what normal stuff does your grandmother not want you to do?"

"Well, for starters instead of letting me hang out with my friends, she wants me to come here, that's not normal, is it? She knows that I don't want to come here, but she just keeps saying that I need to. Normal is not coming to talk to your pastor about stuff that is nobody's business. Not normal." Zarina said in a louder tone than she had intended.

After a moment, she started again, "Why can't she just leave me alone?"

"Why do you think your grandmother wants to monitor where you go and what you do?"

"I don't know."

"Is that really true? Don't you know why she is concerned about you?"

"She had no right to tell you, you know. No right at all."

"Our first meeting we talked about that remember? We all agreed - your grandmother, you and I. We all talked about this and I thought that we all agreed that we everyone could share their thoughts and concerns and that everything said during our session would be confidential, right? You agreed during that session that she could share her concerns with me. Is that right?"

"Yes, but I felt like she was going to tell you whether I wanted her to or not. So I didn't feel like I had much choice but to agree."

"I am sorry that you felt that way. Does it help you at all to know that our conversations are confidential?"

"Yes, that is the only reason that I am talking to you at all."

Trying to get back on track Rev. Branford said, "So your grandmother is concerned with who you are going out with."

"No, she is concerned that I have not told him that I have the virus, so he could drop me like a hot rock. She wants me to be all alone, sitting around watching Wheel of Fortune with her forever and ever. She would love that. Poor little Zarina." Zarina began imitating her grandmother's voice and shaking her head from side to side, "I have to take care of her because she is too stupid to take care of herself."

"Is that really what you think that your grandmother thinks?"

"Yes, she doesn't care about me. All she ever says is, 'Have you told him yet? Have you told him yet? Have you told him yet?' She is not thinking about me at all. She is only thinking about herself. My grandma said as much herself when she said, 'Zarina, I know how boys are at the prom and everything. If something happens between the two of you, and he gets sick, what will people think about me? You have to tell him so he won't try anything.' Who cares what people think about her? What about me? She is supposed to protect me."

Zarina slumped silently in the leather chair, staring blankly at her pastor while she tried to keep her mind focused on how pretty she would look at the prom.

It seemed to the pastor that she went from a teen angel to a tormented adult in the few seconds it took to ask the question, 'What about me'.

"Zarina do you know why it is important to your grandmother that you tell your friend that you have HIV?" he asked.

Pressing her lips so tightly together they seemed to disappear into her face, "it is not fair," Zarina said as she fondled the cut out picture of her prom dress. "Why should I have to tell him? Nobody told me!" she screamed and folded her face into her hands allowing hot tears to distort the picture she was holding. "Nobody told me!"

Rev. Branford allowed a few seconds of silence to hang like a heavy mist between Zarina's response, and his slowly asked question, "Zarina, are you saying that the person that you got the virus from did not tell you that he was infected or are you saying that no one told you how you could get infected?" Rev. Branford handed the young girl a tissue giving her a chance to collect her thoughts.

"Thank you," she said using the tissue to blow her nose. Composing herself Zarina said, "I meant that the person that gave me the virus never said anything about it. Not even after they found out that I got sick, too. Nothing. No, I'm sorry. Nothing," she said as more tears flowed down her checks.

"How does that make you feel?

"How do you think it makes me feel?" she snarled through clinched teeth. "It makes me mad and don't you even begin to try to talk to me again about forgiveness because there is no way I can ever forgive the person who did this to me. I will hate him until I die and thanks to this disease that might not be too long, but as long as I breathe I will hate him."

"Would you want someone to hate you the way that you hate the person that gave you the virus?"

"You sound like my grandmother. Why is everyone so concerned about the people I am friends with?

You think they are so great, and you don't want them to end up like me, right? Is that it? Why, shouldn't they? Give me one good reason why I should care."

In a more haltering voice, Zarina continued, "I thought that if I stayed a virgin I did not have to worry about anything, and I never thought of myself as anything but a virgin because I had never been with a boy in a sexual way, at least not in a way that I thought of as sexual." Stuttering just a little she said, "I am not a bad person or a wild girl I was just doing what all of my friends were doing, guys and girls. We didn't think that it was a bad thing or anything like that. It was just something to do. It wasn't even real sex; I mean it was just like kissing except it was somebody's private parts. Tell me, why this had to happen to me, please. Please just tell me that."

Rev. Branford thought to himself for a long time. Finally, he looked at Zarina and said, "Darling, I don't know why you got HIV when so many others who have done the same thing as you have not.

Only God knows the answer to that question. I do know that hurting other people is never a way to deal with our pain or our disappointments in life. We can't deal with our problems that way."

"You don't understand, Pastor, I am not trying to hurt anybody, but I would rather kill myself than have anybody know that I am HIV positive. I might as well be dead. No one would want to be friends with me if they knew. I would be all alone." Then she said in a quiet almost stifled voice, "I am not even sure if my parents did not send me away because they did not want to be around me. Why is it so hard for my grandmother to get it? I just want to be normal."

Could it be because she wants what is best for you?

I don't know." she replied. Desperately wanting to change the subject Zarina said, "Pastor did I tell you who I am going to the prom with?"

"No, I don't think that you did."

"Samuel Leigh," she said very proudly.

"I'm sorry, who?" Rev. Branford said, wanting her to confirm what he thought he heard.

"You know, Junior, Junior Leigh.   He goes here. His mom is Samantha Leigh she sings in the choir."

"Oh, yes, yes." Rev. Branford's true reactions were constrained by his conversation with Samantha Leigh earlier in the day. "Is he excited about going to the prom?" he asked.

"Sure. I mean he is about as excited as most boys are about getting dressed up and going to a dance, but he seems to be okay with it."

"So, is Junior the person your grandmother wants you to tell that you have HIV?

"Yes, but I am not going to do that. I don't think that I should have to tell him anything."

"I know that this might sound like a strange question, but I was wondering what you think you would have done differently if you had known in advance that the person you were with was HIV positive?

There was silence in the room as Zarina, mulled the question over for a minute and then said, "I've thought about it a lot, and the truth is that I don't really know. I don't know if I understood what it really meant to have HIV. I just thought that if I stayed a virgin I did not have to worry about anything, and I never thought of myself as anything but a virgin because I had never been with a boy, in a sexual, way at least not in a way that I thought of as sexual."

"How about now, Zarina, now that you do know. What would you do differently?"

"I am not sure. I, I don't know," she stammered. "When I first came to live with my grandparents, I just wanted to forget about everything that had happened. It was my chance to start over. I wanted to fit in with the other kids and not have anybody know about my situation. Most of all I wanted to stop being scared all of the time," she paused and stared at the floor. "I don't think I would want anybody to feel scared the way I do all of the time."

"Scared? Of people rejecting you because of your disease?"

"Yes," she picked her head up. "So, I tried to do what I thought people expected me to do. I study hard and make good grades so that everyone can be proud of me. I have friends. I take my medicines and eat right. I do everything I am supposed too. I just want to be normal."

"And your relationship with Junior, does that help to make you feel normal?"

"Yes. It makes me feel like I am a normal teenager."

"Do you care about him?"

"Sure, he has been very nice to me."

"Zarina, your grandmother says that you are seeing a therapist to help you deal with the stress of living with HIV, but she wanted me to talk to you about the moral issues of living with HIV. Is that okay with you?"

"I'm here, right?" Zarina snapped.

"I understand that you don't really want to be here, and that is okay but may I ask you another question?"

"I don't care."

"What do you think is the right thing to do?" Branford said putting emphasis on the word right. "Do you believe that you should you tell Junior that you are HIV positive or not? I want you to think about it before you answer because you've already told me what you want to do. Now I want to know what you believe is the right thing to do."

"Let me ask you a question, you asked me if I cared about Junior, but you never asked me if I cared about myself. If you had asked me that; then I would have told you yes. I care about Junior, but I care about me more. I care about me more than anything or anyone else. I want to be normal, and I want to be happy. So until somebody figures out how to make that happen with me telling everybody that I am HIV positive, I am not going to tell anybody anything."

"Thank you for being honest," Pastor Branford said as 1 Corinthian 13:11 flashed through his head, "When I was a child, I spoke as a child; I understood as a child, I thought as a child."

"I want you to remember something that no matter how many people turn their backs on you either because of your disease or anything else, God will always be with you. Will you remember that for me?"

"Sure, Pastor Branford," Zarina hesitated then asked "Do you think that God still loves me?"

"Of course I do. In fact, I know that He does. The real question is do you love Him?"

"I don't know if I love him, Pastor. I know that I am supposed to. Sometimes I really want to. But I don't know if I really do."

Before he could respond, Zarina continued. "Pastor, I don't want you to think that I am mean, evil or crazy. I am not. I found out that I tested positive for HIV when I was fourteen - my freshman year of high school. I wasn't sick or anything. One night my Mom got a call from the mother of a girlfriend of mine asking if I had been tested. Before I could figure out what was going on, my Mom was all over me, crying, yelling and screaming for my father. The next day, she took me to a Planned Parenthood office a few towns over from where we lived so that I could be tested. She didn't want anybody to know about it. When the results came back from the test, my parents stopped talking to me for a few days. It was like I didn't exist or something. Finally we went to my doctor, and he explained to me what was going on in my body and what to expect."

"I'm sorry they reacted that way."

"It was okay after they finally got over the shock. But just when things were getting back to normal I had a nose bleed in school. My homeroom teacher started yelling for everybody to get back like I was some kind of deranged ax murderer about to chop off somebody's head. I was sent home from school because I had blood on my clothes. That was on a Wednesday by Friday even my best friend since kindergarten would not talk to me. I spent the rest of the year sitting by myself at lunch. For months afterwards I would wake up from hearing my teacher screaming, "Get away from her." Before that, I had a lot of friends. After that, I was not invited to one party, sleepover or anything else for the rest of the year. At the end of the school year, my parents put me into a private school and prayed that nothing bad would happen. Things were going okay until my father lost his job. The company he worked for moved to another state. A few months later, my parents couldn't afford to pay my tuition anymore. Eventually, my parents sent me to live with my grandparents. Everybody said that I could have a normal life here. No one here would know about my condition. I was happy to come."

"I met Junior here at the church my first weekend here. My grandma brought me to the Back to School Youth Revival, and she introduced me to a group of kids there. He and I hit it off right away. My grandma didn't seem to have any problem with our friendship until he asked me to go to the prom with him. At first she said that she didn't want me to go. She said that she didn't want me to go because the prom is for seniors and I am only a junior. I told her that plenty of juniors go to the prom. So, when that excuse for keeping me from going to the prom did not work, my grandma said, 'You can only go to the prom if you tell Junior that you are HIV positive.' When I told her that I did not want to tell him, she said that either I tell him before the prom or she will tell Junior herself. She says that she can't let him take me to the prom without knowing the truth. I know that she is only being this way because she thinks something will happen. Even though I've told her a hundred times that nothing would. She makes me so mad. This is so unfair. I don't want him to hate me and I am tired of hating myself. My life is ruined, and I am only sixteen. Why would God do this to me? I think that Junior will be ashamed to be my friend. He would never want to take me to the prom as his date. I think that he will hate me. No one will ever want to have me as a date, will they? What did I do? Do you think Junior will hate me when he finds out? I will always be alone, won't I?" Zarina was firing questions so fast Rev. Branford could not keep up.

Finally, Zarina stopped questioning him, Branford thought I can't say to a sixteen year old that you brought this on yourself, not God so; he asked in an emphatic voice instead, "Are planning to tell Junior about your situation, Zarina?"

A look of absolute resolve covered Zarina face. The pasted smile and thoughts of a fun night at the prom were long gone. Silence crept into the office like a thief in the night sucking the youth from Zarina before Branford's eyes. "I don't know, she mumbled. I feel hurt that my grandmother thinks that I would have sex with Junior knowing that I have HIV, without telling him. I am tired of telling her that nothing will happen. I thought that she loved me, and trusted me. But she doesn't. She just thinks I am a stupid girl who sleeps around with everybody. I know that I made a mistake, but that doesn't mean that I am not a good person. I just made a mistake."

In a shrill voice that pierced Branford's heart Zarina screeched, "Everybody makes mistakes. I just made a mistake. I just want to get to normal."

Taking a deep breath Rev. Branford tried to reassure Zarina without being patronizing, "That is true. We do all make mistakes and once we have acknowledged our mistakes we should be allowed to move forward. You are right about that." Thinking about his own past, Branford lost focus on the young girl seated in front of him for a moment.

Zarina stated again, "The truth is that I told Junior that I wanted to stay a virgin until I got married. He thinks that is great. He thinks I am this good girl who really believes in God, the Bible, and the whole nine yards. He would never try to do anything to change my mind about that. He is too nice a guy for that."

"Are you saying that the two of you are really just friends not girlfriend and boyfriend?"

"Yes, Junior wants to concentrate on school, and he is working hard to get good grades so that he can get into college. When he tells his friends that he can't hang out with them; he sort of blames it on me. It's a lot easier than saying that he has to go home, and do his homework. This works for both of us. He gets to spend his time studying, and I don't feel left out and alone. We go to the movies and hang out sometimes but just as friends."

"Did you tell your grandmother about this arrangement?"

"No."

"Why not?"

"Because I want her to trust me because she loves me, and she should know me. I know that I made a mistake before, but that was all that it was - a mistake. I am not crazy, evil or stupid. I like that Junior thinks that I am this really good person. He doesn't feel sorry for me. He isn't afraid of me. He just accepts me for who he thinks I am, and I want it to stay that way. I just want it to be normal between us. Besides, there are just a few more weeks until school is over. Junior will graduate and then he will be away at college. If my grandma doesn't ruin it for me. I will still be able to say that we are seeing each other, and everything will work out. You see, don't you? If she just leaves everything alone and stops meddling, everything will be fine. I just wish that everybody would let me work things out my own way."

"If Junior is truly your friend do you think that you could trust him to keep your secret?"

"Pastor, I trusted my grandmother to keep it and you see where that got me. In other words no, N. O.," emphasizing each letter in the word. "I don't want to take a chance and tell anyone. Half of the crap on the internet is there because somebody's friend that they trusted put it there. So no."

Thinking about it again, a little half smile came over her face, "Maybe someday. I hope someday. But for now I am not ready for any kind of real relationship with a guy. I don't know if that will ever happen but for now, no, I don't want to tell anyone."

"Zarina, do you know the story of Queen Esther in the Bible?

"No, not really."

"Well, she was a young Jewish girl. She may have been around your age when she was chosen to become the wife of the king, King Xerxes."

"I don't mean to be rude but what does that have to do with me? I am not trying to marry Junior. Didn't you understand what I said? We are just friends," Zarina interrupted the Pastor's story.

"I understood you. Just hear me out for a minute. You see, Esther also had a secret, one that she kept from everyone around her, including her husband, the king."

"Really, what was it?" she queried.

"Yes, she hid the fact that she was Jewish from everyone around her including her husband. But one day something happened and she had to make a decision about whether or not she would tell her secret in order to help her people. Orphaned as a young girl, Esther's cousin Mordecai raised her as his own daughter after her parents died. The Bible says that Esther was lovely, and beautiful. I like to think that her spirit was lovely, the way she presented herself to the world was lovely and her face was a reflection of what was inside of her, it was beautiful. So she was lovely and beautiful.

"At some point, Mordecai learned of King Xerxes' decree that all of the young virgin women in his kingdom were to be gathered up and brought to his harem and that he would select a new queen from these young women. Knowing that Esther would be among the young women taken to the harem, Mordecai instructed her not to tell anyone about her heritage. She was not to tell anyone that she was

Jewish while she was in the king's household. So, she never did. Not even when she was selected by the king, to become his wife and queen."

"Why didn't he want her to tell anyone that she was Jewish?"

"Well, I can imagine that he did not want her to have any trouble. Mordecai must have felt that if people knew that Esther was Jewish some people might not treat her very nicely. Mordecai loved her and wanted her to be accepted by the people in charge of the harem, much like your parents, in your situation. Your Mom and Dad want you to experience every good thing about being a teenager. Right? They probably have even encouraged you to keep your condition a secret because they don't want you shunned by the kids at your school or treated any differently than any of the other kids. Is that right?"

"Yes, I understand now," Zarina said bobbing her head quickly up and down.

Rev. Branford continued, "One day her cousin Mordecai sent her a note telling her that her husband the king had signed a decree at the suggestion of one of his noblemen that would in effect allow for the annihilation of all of the Jewish people in his kingdom. Mordecai was devastated by the king's action, and Mordecai asked Esther to go to the king to beg for mercy. He begged her to plead for the lives of their people. This news caused several problems for Esther, not the least of which was that she could lose her position in the kingdom, maybe even her own life if she told her husband that she was Jewish. She did not know what her husband's reaction would be. Not only that, but unlike in our society where husbands and wives live with other, and usually see each other every day; although she was the queen, she would only have contact with her husband when he summoned her. The story says that King Xerxes had not summoned Esther for thirty days before she got this news from Mordecai.

Because their contact was so sporadic, the only way for Queen Esther to see her husband was to go to him while he was holding court with the subjects of his kingdom. The king's policy was if any person came into the inner court without prior permission, unless the king raised his scepter and approved their appearance before him, the person would be put to death. Can you imagine what she must have thought when Mordecai asked her to go to her husband and tell him her secret?

"Yes, I live it every day."

"I know. Can you guess what she did?"

"Sure, it's a Bible story so she must have told him, and everything worked out fine right?"

"Yes, in a sense, however, everything was not that simple. I want you to think about what I just said. Here, is a young girl who has suffered the heartbreak of having both of her parents die. She is being raised by her cousin Mordecai, and although he treats her like she is his daughter and they love each other very much, I am sure that she misses her mother and her father. You can understand that right?"

"Sure, I miss my Mom and Dad, too. I am glad that they are not dead like Esther's but being away from them is hard."

"I can imagine that it is," Rev. Branford said as he continues the story. "Now, King Xerxes decides to snatch her and all of the young virgins in his province away from their families, their friends, and the people they know and bring them to his harem. No place in the story does it say that this is what Esther or any of the young girls wanted. 'You are going,' is what they were told, and it is what they did. The king did not care about their feelings or their dreams for their own lives. It did not matter what they may have wanted to do with their lives or what plans their families may have had for them. They were required to go, and they went. They went for the express purpose of being available for King

205

Xerxes to select a queen from among them. These young women were sent to the king to provide him with entertainment and sex. Sure, we can make it sound glamorous but honestly think about it. Suppose the governor of this state were to sign a law that gave him permission to have every young woman at age fourteen brought to the capital building and held captive there because he wanted to have sex with them. Despite the law, most people would still call him a kidnapper and a rapist, right?"

"Sure would, and that is not all we would call him! That would be crazy."

"So you see what I mean? Things are seldom as simple as they seem at first," Rev. Branford laughed at her response. "Zarina," he asked. "Can you see how the media through its advertising and the world in general today is telling young girls that it's what they are here for, the entertainment of men and boys and for sex? Young girls like you are having sex before they are really ready to because the world is telling them that is what they must do it to be popular and to be accepted by their peers. We know that Esther became Queen, but think about all of the young women whose lives were ruined by the king. Think of what happened to all of the young women who remained in the harem as property of the king. Girls not chosen were devastated I am sure. Can you imagine the tears they cried knowing there was no hope of fulfilling their dreams? They were not unlike many young girls today who after having sex find that they simply feel used, dirty and unlovable. Today after being robbed of the precious gift of virginity, young girls are left unable to fulfill their dreams or reach their full potential because they are saddled with children, diseases and low self-esteem.

"I told you this story Zarina because there is a question that Mordecai asked Esther before she made her decision to tell the king, that I want to ask you.

"What was it?"

"Mordecai asked her, 'who knows whether you have come to the kingdom for such a time as this?'" Branford quoted the Bible from Esther 4:14.

"I am not sure what that means. What does a kingdom have to do with me? Why are you asking me this?"

"I just wondered if you had ever thought about how many young girls in the high school, in the community, even in this church you could save by sharing your story?"

"Save?"

"Yes. When we first started talking you told me that nobody told you about how you could get this disease, but then you changed your mind about that, and you said that you were told, you just didn't take it seriously. You didn't understand or believe that it could happen to you. I wonder if you had heard from a young girl your own age that she was infected with HIV and that she got it from having oral sex;

would that have made the possibility of you getting the virus more real to you? If the person who was talking to you had been someone you could relate to instead of an adult Sex Education Teacher, your parents, even your Pastor would you have taken the threat of getting the virus more seriously. Do you think you would have understood better that this could actually happen to you? Would you have given more thought to what you were doing and made different decisions?"

"I don't know, maybe." Zarina sighed at the thought and shrugged her shoulders.

"I also wonder if you shared your story if there wouldn't be some young girl who takes you seriously and maybe even not take the risks that you did without thinking about it. I wonder what if you were meant to save your people, your peers by sharing your secret. What if you were meant to use your situation as a means of helping others, just by sharing your story?"

"But my friends will hate me. No one will want to be around me. They will be scared of me."

"Do you want to know what Esther said when she had to make her decision?"

"What?"

"'And so I will go to the king, which is against the law; and if I perish, I perish!'" he quoted from Esther 4:16. Esther had to decide that no matter what happened to her, she must help her people. Even if, you had to miss a party or two, but you could save someone's life, would it be worth it?"

"I don't know. You make it sound so easy, like a fairy tale or something but this is my real life and it doesn't seem that easy to me."

"I know, Zarina. You will find as you grow up that very little that really matters in life is easy. Nevertheless you get to choose just like Esther did. You can do what is easy or to take a chance and do what is hard. You can hide your secrets and live behind lies, or you can take a chance and reveal you secrets and possibly save many people from making grave mistakes. Do you know how many teenage girls like yourself expose themselves to HIV; STD's, and unwanted pregnancies? They are your peers. They are your people. Have you considered helping them? That is the real question. Instead of seeing this as a curse, it can be seen as an opportunity to be a blessing. You can bless so many people just by allowing your story to be told. As we mature, we begin to stop thinking so much about ourselves and to think about others. Sure Esther could have kept quiet. No one except her cousin knew about her background. She may have escaped being killed, and she knew all of that as she thought about and prayed about what she would do. Eventually, she decided that she cared more about others and helping them than she did about her own safety and well-being."

"I see. So that is what you want me to do. You want me to care more about other people than I do about myself?"

"Only if that is what you believe is the right thing to do."

"So if I don't then I am a terrible person, right?" She responded with anger.

"No, I did not say that. I don't walk in your shoes. I can't tell you what it is that God would have you to do. I can only point you in the direction that I think He would have you to go. God allows each of us to make choices. This is a choice that you will have to make. There is another part of the story that we did not talk about. She prayed about her decision before she made it and she asked others to pray for her, as well. She was not alone. You are not alone either. The people who really love and care about you will continue to love and care about you. Those people who don't continue to care about you were not your real friends and did not really love you to begin with.

"I want you to read the entire book of Esther and think and pray about what you would like to do about telling Junior and maybe even others. If you want to talk to someone confidentially from our HIV Ministry, let me know. Most of all I want you to know that no matter what you decide I will support you." Branford stopped for a moment then asked, "Zarina, you do you know my daughters?"

"Yes, we've met at the Youth meeting. Abigail seems shy, and your son Jai is a little quiet, but your daughter, Penny certainly is not. She is a total riot."

"Yes, I know," he said thinking about Penny for a minute then turning his attention back to Zarina and the real question that he had in mind. "Abigail is thirteen, she will be fourteen in a month, and I was thinking about the kind of impact you would have on her if you spoke to her about your experiences. How you came to make the decision to have sex. You could talk to her about peer pressure or whatever else contributed to your decision?"

"I understand."

"I am going to give you a reading assignment to complete for me for our next meeting. Will you do that for me?"

"Sure."

"Okay, may I pray with you?"

Chapter 4: The Results Are In

Rev. Branford greeted Clarissa with a jovial "Good morning" as he made his way up the hall. "I noticed that you finally took my advice and closed the window blinds." He began teasing Clarissa before he saw Samantha and a man he assumed to be her husband sitting in the waiting area outside of his office along with her son.

"Oh, hi Samantha" he said as he extended his arm to shake her outstretched hand, recalling the details of his meeting with Samantha the previous week and wondering if something had gone wrong.

"Pastor, this is my husband, Samuel, and you know Junior," she said turning to the man sitting next to her. Standing she continued hurriedly, "Clarissa said that it was okay to wait for you here. We need to talk to you. Can you see us now?"

"Sure, come on in," Rev. Branford said as he unlocked his office door.

"It is nice to finally meet you Samuel. Please come on in and have a seat." The couple followed Rev. Branford into his office. The three seated themselves in the cattycorner leather chairs facing the desk. "A nice looking family," Branford thought to himself.

"It is nice to finally be able to meet you, too," said Samuel. "Samantha told me about your conversation with her last week. She said that you suggested that we both take the HIV test."

"Yes, I did. Did you agree with my suggestion?"

"Yes, after I thought about it for a while. We both wanted to thank you for suggesting that we get tested." Samuel emphasized the word "we" in his sentence.

"Oh, no problem," the pastor said trying to force a smile to his face. "Did everything work out alright for the two of you?"

"Actually, for the three of us. Junior insisted on driving to pick up his father and taking him to the doctor. After a little arm-twisting, he decided to take the test with us, although, we were not really worried about Junior especially. He is seeing that sweet little Adams girl, Zarina, you know. And none of us were positive for HIV. I am glad to report." Samantha said hurriedly.

"Great," the pastor said. Samantha could never have imagined how immensely relieved Rev. Branford was to hear the news particularly about Junior. "So what brings you in today?"

"We want to renew our vows," Samuel said with a big Cheshire Cat grin on his face.

"Sure, we can set that up. Do you have a date in mind?"

"Yes, today," said Samuel looking at Samantha.

"Today, if it is possible," Samantha confirmed.

"Today it is," Rev. Branford said, "Do you want to do it right now?

"Is seven o'clock this evening okay with you, Pastor?" asked Samantha.

"Sure," Rev. Branford said, thinking of another canceled dinner with his family. "Do you want to do it in my office, the chapel or the sanctuary?"

"Your office is fine. It is just going to be the three of us," Samantha said.

"Dad, are we going to dinner after the ceremony?"

"Whatever your Mom wants to do," Samuel answered patting his wife's hand.

"Sure. Pastor you are invited if you would like to come," Samantha answered.

'Oh, thank you, maybe some other time. I promised Penny I would help her with her homework tonight."

"I'm sorry. We never thought about your schedule. We can do it tomorrow I guess if that is better for you," Samantha responded.

"No, it is fine. My wife will cover it, as long as I get there before her bedtime it will be fine." Remembering the floor full of toys trap Penny had recently set to catch him coming into her room after her bed time.

"Can I invite Zarina? She is very excited about the wedding," asked Junior.

"Sure. She can come if her grandparents say that it is okay."

"Pastor, don't tell Zarina that I told you this, but on Monday she wants to meet with you to discuss some project or something. She wants me to come with her to talk to you. She did not give me many of the details when I spoke to her this afternoon. We didn't have long to talk. My Mom kept interrupting me about the wedding while I was trying to talk to her.

And, even though she said that she wasn't, she seemed concerned about how you would respond to whatever it is that she wants to do. I guess that she wants me to come along with her for moral support. She may have already made the appointment, I'm not sure. But I do know that she wants it to happen on Friday. So I will be here with her. Maybe she will tell me more about it tonight at dinner," Junior said.

"Junior, tonight will be too special a night to get bogged down in church projects," Branford said in a voice an octave higher than he would have liked. "Why don't you just enjoy your parents' wedding? Let Zarina surprise both of us on Friday."

Chapter 5: Questions

Rev. Joshua Branford could feel himself beginning to relax as he approached the intersection of English Street and Spring Lane. He was already adjusting his attitude from being Rev. Branford to being Daddy, from counselor to husband, supervisor to partner as he approached his house. Driving by slowly, the branches of the trees along the streets seemed to sway like gigantic arms bidding him welcome while the aging Victorian style houses that loomed behind the trees seemed stoic but inviting. Many of the houses were painted soft shades of beige, baby blue and green. They had triangular gables, large protruding bay windows and entrances with decorative white columns, but not his. The Branford house was a four bedroom, white farmhouse. Except that there were no chickens running around the front yard, it could have passed for the house, he saw in old black and white photographs of his great grandparents standing, smiling, and waving as one or more of their children left home in search of a better life in the big city. His wife had fallen in love with the house on their first visit to the city. "It's so quaint," she told him and "I just love all of the room." He believed that if the truth were told, she liked it so much because she envisioned having several quiet places to hide from Penny, their youngest and devilishly rambunctious daughter. He had preferred something a little more modern, less expensive and a lot closer to the church, but because she had been so sweet about uprooting their children and moving when he was asked to be the pastor of Hope and Grace Christian Center he could not help but say yes to the house. But, over the months, he had come to love it too, particularly now that it had what he called an office and what his wife called a man-cave. It was just a little space that he had carved out for himself in the basement behind the plumbing and hot water heater.

The house also had wood burning fireplaces in the living room, family room and master bedroom, a wraparound porch, and the generous backyard was enclosed by a white picket fence. On nice days, when he got home on time, he and the kids would break out the barbeque and basketball. But tonight was Friday. Friday was always the night that he would practice his sermon before his captive audience, his family. Jai, his son called it Freak Out Friday because he never knew when his father was going to use one of them or some other family member as an example in his sermon. Jai hated to hear his name called from the pulpit, the thought of Jai's brown face turning red from embarrassment made Joshua smile to himself.

Just as easily as the smile had crossed Joshua's face, his thoughts turned irrepressibly to the people he had counseled during the week. Joshua desperately wished he knew how they were making the decisions that had the potential of changing their lives forever. In his mind, he replayed the scriptures that he would recite on Sunday, in his sermon "What's Next" for the umpteenth time. Wanting to be perfect in his delivery, he implored God to allow the sermon to help people make not only good, but Godly decisions. Joshua wanted to influence the people he counseled, as well as the congregation.

However, as usual he was unsure of himself. His sermons never felt good enough and most importantly his ability to preach with power and conviction always seemed to be lacking, despite what others said to reassure him. He hated the overwhelming sense of unworthiness more than anything else. Insecurity followed him like a shadow whenever the lights were on; and, when he stood before the congregation, there it was reminding him of his own failings. "Why me?" Joshua frequently asked God. He was still waiting for an answer.

As Joshua journeyed, additional questions rolled through his head like carhops on skates. How is Kitera making the choice of whether or not to attend Diondra's trial? Would she pray about it and listen to God's voice? If she decided to go to Diondra's trial would she plead with the judge for leniency for the teenaged girl accused of killing her daughter, a girl that she once cared for like a daughter? Had she truly forgiven Diondra and even if she had forgiven her, would she still want Diondra punished for what happened? After all, like she said, her daughter is dead because of Diondra. Did she believe that Diondra should have had control over her emotions no matter what? Would her standards be higher for Diondra than Danni? The questions flowed like a rushing river.

His thoughts were not just about Kitera and Diondra, but about Dean, Diondra's brother. He tried to imagine what life was like for the young man who had tried to commit suicide after the death of his girlfriend and baby. How, at such a young age, had Dean come to the conclusion that his life was not worth living? Was Dean emotionally stable now? How would he manage the sentencing hearing for Diondra, his sister? Would the hearing inflict more emotional distress on the teenagers, Dean and Diondra? Would it be more than either could handle?

Joshua's mood darkened further by the thought of the kinds of plans Dean and even Diondra could be making for themselves and their future. Would they ever forgive themselves for Danni's death?

As Joshua trekked along the tree lined street he began to pray again for the parents of Diondra and Dean. He imagined their weariness from carrying the weight of their children's predicaments on their shoulders. The guilt and the sorrow of all of the parents involved had to be weighing heavily on all of them. Kitera was concerned about her daughter's eternal life, which she no longer could have any effect on, but Dean and Diondra's parents were concerned about their children's future. They were still living and could be saved, but how? How to make things better for their children must have been in the forefront of their thoughts. How could they release their pain? How could he support them all, he wondered? Would he be able to them get the help they needed?

Joshua's mood lifted a little as he recalled his conversation with Samantha. He was thankful to God for the negative HIV reports that the members of the Leigh family received. Samantha, Samuel and Junior all seemed happy about their reunion, but he also wondered what was next for them. How would they adjust to being back together as a family, living under one roof? What would happen after the newness of Samuel's release wore off? Would Samuel fit in as the head of the household? Had Samantha sincerely forgiven him for being locked-up? What kind of relationship would he have now with his sister, nieces, and mother? Would Junior be respectful of a flawed father, a felon out on parole? Would Samuel's adjustment to life outside of prison be an easy one or would he become another recidivism statistic? He shuddered to think how Junior would feel later, when he thought about the reason his parents wanted to be tested for HIV. Only time would tell what was next for this family.

Finally, Joshua's thoughts turned to Zarina. His heart truly went out to her. How difficult it must be for a young girl her age, to wrestle with the day-to-day ordeal of living with a life threatening illness. Add to that the torment of being ostracized by family and friends because of it; he could not imagine the suffering she had already endured. Joshua didn't know if he should dread the upcoming meeting on Monday with Zarina and Junior because of the possibility that she would decide not to share information about her condition with anyone.

Or if he would be happy that she had decided to share information about her condition. More importantly, Joshua wondered if he were actually ready for the responsibility of helping Zarina weather the storm that would inevitably result from her actions. No matter which scenario followed, Joshua was concerned about how Zarina was making her decision.

"What will Zarina do, is the million dollar question?" Branford said out loud to himself as the lush green grass in his own yard finally came into view. A sense of peacefulness again washed over him. Grateful for the sight of his gravel-paved driveway, his family, and even (he had to admit to himself) for his role as a pastor in the lives of the members of Hope and Grace. He smiled again as he thought about the fact that when it came to his brood he never knew what was coming next.

Joshua banked his car left and crept into the driveway, trying to avoid Jai's bicycle, which was lying directly in his path. He could already hear Ebony, their dog, barking at the door before he put his key into the keyhole. He knew that Penny would not be far behind.

"Daddy, Daddy guess what?" Penny shouted in her usual excited voice just as he stepped inside the door.

"Don't I even get a hello, before I have to start guessing?"

"Yes, sure Daddy, hello. Now, guess what?"

"What, Penny? But before I guess, tell me is it a good or a bad, guess what?"

"Um, I am not sure. I think that it is good, but I think that Mom thinks that it is bad."

"Okay, give me a hint."

"Oh, Daddy. Just listen to this. You know the guppy that you bought me last Saturday, the one in my room in the little fish bowl."

"Yessssss," Joshua said slowly.

"Well it is a mommy." Penny shouted.

"Oh, okay. That is good, right?"

"I thought so, but I don't think Mommy thinks so."

"Why not?"

"Because Daddy, listen to this: the guppy had thirty-seven babies at one time."

"Are you sure?"

"Yes, Jai and I counted them and guess what else? After she had the babies, she jumped out of the bowl. Jai said it was like she was trying to kill herself or something."

"Thirty-seven guppies?"

"Yes, and Mommy said that if she had thirty-seven babies at one time she would try to kill herself, too."

"Can you believe that, Daddy?"

"I guess so… I mean about the fish, not your Mom."

"So now we need a new tank and an air pump, and of course more food for all of those guppies. Can we go to the pet store and get the stuff after dinner?"

"I suppose so."

"Are we doing Freak Out Friday tonight Daddy?"

"Yes, my sermon is ready."

"Can you make it short? Please, Daddy? You know once you get going the pet store will be closed before you finish."

"Pen, you sound like one of my members. Go tell Jai to move his bicycle out of the driveway, please.

"Ok."

"Where is your Mom?"

"She's in the kitchen."

"Is she frying fish?"

"Yuck, Daddy! Noooo, you are gross sometimes you know." She said as she stomped off.

Joshua smiled and thought, "Grossing my kids out. All must be right with the world."

Sermon: What's Next?
Genesis 8:16-22

Have ups and downs in your life ever caused you to wonder, "What's next?" I mean, have you ever been in a situation when you could not help but ask "Lord, what is next?" Well, imagine being Noah and hearing God tell you that He was going to destroy every living breathing thing in the world. There will be no exceptions. Everything except Noah and his family will be washed away in a flood. Can you imagine Noah not wondering "What's next?" I certainly cannot.

I had a "what's next" experience on September 11, 2001. I got off of the subway in New York City, two stops from the World Trade Center. The weather was warm for a September day, and the sky was a perfect mix of blue and white. I walked the few blocks to my office, stopping only to grab a banana nut muffin from my favorite vending truck. When I arrived at my office building, I took the elevator to the 13th floor. Once in my office I was amazed by what I saw. Out of my wall length window I could see the tail of a plane sticking out of the World Trade Center. It was hard for me to believe what I was seeing. Having no doubt that this must have been an unfortunate accident I decided to go down to the corner store and buy a camera so that I could take a picture to show my children, knowing they would never believe me if I simply told him that a plane had flown into the tall and extremely avoidable tower of the World Trade Center. In fact, I did not believe what I was seeing myself, and I was staring directly at it.

A few minutes later as I came out of the store, I saw a woman kneeling down on the sidewalk. She was crying. Others were pointing up at the World Trade Center. They had followed the route of the low flying second plane as it flew into the second tower. As you can probably imagine, it was a terrifying day, to say the least. Everyone wanted to know "What is going on. What's happening?" Even more importantly, most were asking the question of others and of God, "What's next?"

Yet, even after seeing the plane sticking out of the building and watching with tears in my eyes as the twin towers fell, one of the things that had the greatest impact on me about that day was not the planes, nor seeing the soldiers on the streets of New York City in full combat mode carrying machine guns, or the silence of the usually busy and bustling streets. What impacted me most on 9-11 was finally walking into my parents' home that night and having my mother who is one of the strongest persons that I know fall into my arms and cry like a baby. She kept repeating over and over, "Thank you, God. Thank you, God. Thank you." She kept crying out, simply, "thank you" to her God and mine.

My mom was uncharacteristically emotional, unabashedly grateful, and unashamedly thankful because you see all day long she like many others had been asking the question, "What's next?" She wanted to know what in the world is going to happen next. Would there be more attacks? Would there be more lives lost? Would love ones make it home safely? Would life as we know it, ever be the same? What's next, Lord? Yes, that day for many, like me, my co-workers, even my mother was filled with the question, "What's next?" And for her, when I walked through the door, there was some relief, some semblance of normality, some longed for reminder that God was in control of whatever came next and that God alone could bring us through whatever was next.

Most of us have had one or two, "What's next" experiences and if you have not had one, keep living and I am sure that you will. Someone's "what next" experiences may have occurred when they lost a job unexpectedly, throwing their ability to support themselves and their families entirely out of kilter.

Some of us have had our "what's next" moments when we've lost loved ones. Maybe it was the death of your mother or father, sister or brother, child, spouse or even your best friend that caused you to throw up your hands and ask, "What's next? What do I do now? How am I going to survive this? What's next?"

And for some of us it was the diagnosis of an illness, the thought of how that diagnosis will impact your life and your lifestyle that caused you to ask the question, "What's next? How can I cope with this? How will I make it through this? What will my life be like? I don't have insurance. I can't pay for my treatment. The doctors don't expect me to make it. What will happen to my children, my spouse? Where do I turn? What's next?"

And for some it has been a happy moment that caused a "what's next" question. Maybe it was after the beautiful wedding and exciting honeymoon, when reality begins to set in, and the question of what's next arises or maybe it was after the birth of that much longed for child that the 'what's next question' presents itself. I don't know what caused your "what's next" moment, but whatever it is, you can rest assured that you are not the only one to ever ask the question. You are not the only one to want to know, how do you get through the unexpectedness of life? How do we face our storms? What do you do when the ground beneath you is being shaken to its very core? What do you do when the flood is coming, and you don't have any control over the situation? What do you do when your boat is sinking, and there is no life preserver in sight? What do you do when the water is too rough to swim in and too deep to wade through? When you've asked what's next, and there is no acceptable response? I believe that we ought to look to the Word of God for an answer, if we truly want to know the answer to, "What's Next?"

So today we will look at Noah. We can find Noah as he faces his "What's next" question in Genesis 8:1-22.

Most of us know the story of Noah and the Ark. We know that God instructed Noah to build an ark that would house him and his family along with pairs of animals: those that fly in the sky and those that walk and crawl along the ground. We have all seen the pictures in the children's books of kindly looking old Noah and giraffes and other animals with their heads poking out of the ark. But imagine the real Noah and the seven people with him. Imagine the eight of them knowing that they were going to be the only survivors on the earth. They would become the new Adams and the new Eves, charged with going into this new world, to be fruitful and to multiply.

I can imagine that they wondered and asked "what's next?" as God himself closed the door to the ark. I can hear them with my divinely inspired imagination asking "what's next?" as the ark began to lift off of the ground, to rock and float away. I believe that after they had been floating for weeks during the storm that they might have continued to ask "what's next?"

We might expect that Noah, who the Bible tells us is a righteous man, would feel secure and safe during the flood. After all, God had spoken to him directly, given him a personal overview of what was about to take place. But what about the seven other people that traveled on that ark with Noah - his wife, three sons and their wives? What about these people, the ones the Bible does not call righteous? How did they get through? What must it have been like to be the wife of the youngest son? Perhaps she was the last to join the family, an outsider unfamiliar with Noah and his relationship with God. How strange that family must have seemed to her initially. For she was a person who married into a family like no other on earth, for the Bible says that Noah was a righteous man while all of the humans around him were filled with evil. She left the security of her father's house to live with a man who says that God has spoken to his father (not to him!!!) and that they were going to build an ark, a large boat and live inside it with all kinds of animals. "Why are we building an ark," she might have asked? "Because rain is coming." A storm like no other and everybody on earth is going to be washed away.

Upon hearing this, how fast would you have run away? Keep in mind that in some parts of their world, the rain fall was less than one inch per year. How did she prepare for the flood that was coming into her life? I believe that she learned five things from her father-in-law that helped her get through the storm, to find the answer to "what's next" when her ground was shaky.

She learned first and foremost from her father-in-law to walk with God. Genesis 6:9 says that Noah walked faithfully with God. What does that mean, Preacher?

Well, I am glad that you asked that question. It means that Noah had a connection with God. God was Noah's companion along life's journey. God knew Noah and Noah knew God. They communicated with each other. God spoke to Noah and Noah spoke to God. In other words, the two were in relationship with each other.

If you seriously want to know "what's next," you must get the answer from God. Why? Because God is the only one who knows, without the shadow of a doubt, what is next. You can get counsel from your mother, father, or suggestions from your friends or spouse, but in reality they cannot tell you what's next. You can see a psychic or these days a witch with a crystal ball, but even they cannot tell you what's next. However, God is the Alpha, and the Omega, the beginning and end, the "was and is and is to come." He is the only one who knows what the future holds because He cradles the future in His hands. If you sincerely want to know what's next, you must get the answer from God. You must be in a relationship with God. You must be able to hear His voice and to understand His direction because if God says that a flood is coming, you need to prepare for the deluge; rain is certainly on the way. If God says that your healing is on the way, you don't have to wait until the doctor confirms it, you can shout now because God is not a man. He cannot lie. If you heard from God that your breakthrough is just around the corner, go ahead and celebrate. You can trust in His word. If He tells you to build an ark or start a business, write a book, go back to school, and forgive an enemy or loved one, do it. Even if, your friends all call you crazy, just look them in the face and say with confidence, I can do this without any doubts or fears because God has ordained it. Despite ridicule, Noah did not hesitate to build the ark, and you should not hesitate to do whatever it is that God is asking, telling, and leading you to do. Go forth, conquer, rule, be fruitful, and succeed. Walk with God and He will walk with you.

Second, being with Noah she learned to be patient. She learned to trust God during the storm. In this era of "right now" everything, it is difficult for most of us to be patient. Anything that takes more time to happen than it takes to make popcorn in the microwave is slow, irritating and annoying. We are a "right now" people, and we want a "right now" God - a God who jumps to attention when we speak His name and responds like an app on our phone, instantaneously, when summoned. Let's face it; "right now" people expect a "right now" God.

But if you are going to walk with God you must learn to walk at His pace. You must learn to be patient. Don't get ahead of Him because you might tumble into a pit or get into unforeseen trouble. You might waste time standing on the banks of a river trying to figure out how to get across, never seeing the bridge just around the bend. Or you might climb over a treacherous mountain when an easy to navigate tunnel runs through it. In other words, drugs, sex, or alcohol might begin to look like an answer to your problem because you have left God in your dust. With God out of the picture, low-life living might be your constant companion. Stay in step with God.

And don't fall behind because you might get lost. God may not stay in your sight. You may turn right when you need to turn left. Stealing, suicide or some other self-destructive behavior might seem like the answer. You must be patient and walk at God's pace.

Third, you must trust God. After the storm begins, after the torrential rains began to fall, when the ark was rocking and being battered by the waves, when the winds were blowing, the eight occupants of the ark had to trust God or they probably would have lost their minds. Their trust had to be in God. They had to stay positive to endure the storm and so must we. We must trust in God even when we don't know exactly what is going to happen or why things are happening. We must remind ourselves that we are, at very least, still here. We have not been washed away by the flood. That is not by accident. Remember that God has not brought us this far to leave us now. God has a purpose and a plan for your life. He has already worked everything out in your favor.

Fourth, you must be obedient. God closed the door behind the eight after they entered the ark. He did not leave it up to them to close the door. He knew what was coming. He knew what was next, and He knew what was best. When God closes a door, in your life, it is also because He knows what is coming. He knows what is best, and he knows what is next. The job you lost that you are fretting over will be replaced by something better. The friends that were there while things were going well but who won't return your calls, tweets and have de-friended you on every form of social media, don't give them another thought. That door needed to be closed. The marriage that is in trouble because it was lust not love that caused the union, stop fretting over it. Don't get angry when God closes the door because He has greater plans for you than you have for yourself. Be obedient to God's will.

As the rains began to fall, as people began knocking on the door crying "let me in," the temptation had to be immense to open the door. But they had to be strong; they had to be obedient. Can you hear the cries of the mothers holding their children at the window of the ark begging, not for their own survival but for the life of their children? "Please open the door -- take my baby." Can you hear the rich man offering all that he has to get into the ark or the woman offering up her body to save her life? But the doors of the ark had to remain closed in order for them to complete the task and to receive the blessing that God had prepared for him. They had to be obedient.

The door had to stay closed when the stench of the bodies floating in water mixed with the stench of the animals trapped inside the ark could drive you insane. The door had to stay closed even when they thought God had forsaken them. The door had to stay closed even after the rain stopped. The door even had to stay closed after the sun came out. The door had to stay closed until God was ready for it to be opened. We think of Noah and the forty days and nights of rain, but it actually took more than a year for the waters to recede and for the earth to dry. But the eight were obedient.

They did not open the door. They waited for the Lord, to give them the sign that they could safely leave the ark.

Finally, she learned to give God thanks after the storm. The same thing that I learned from my mother on September 11, she learned from Noah. As soon as I set foot in my parent's house, my mother began to give thanks to God. And as soon as Noah arrived at the beginning of his "what's next," his world after the storm, as soon as he set his feet on solid ground, he gave thanks to God. Noah came out of the ark with his wife, his sons, their wives and the families of animals from the ark and he made an altar and made a sacrifice to the Lord. He did not make a feast for himself and his family. He was not concerned about the scarcity of animals for meat to feed his family. He sacrificed what he had to make his offering, - the animals that had been in the ark with him.

He was not concerned about building a shelter, pleasing his spouse, taking a bath or any other creature comforts. His first action after leaving the ark revealed his true heart -- he made an offering of thanksgiving to the Lord, his God, and his all.

The sacrifice we are told became a sweet aroma to God. God was pleased with the sacrifice. God sent a beautiful rainbow to remind Noah, and us today, of his promise not to destroy humans again with a flood. But not only did God send a rainbow to Noah, later he sent his only begotten son, Jesus Christ into the world. Because Christ came into the world, born of a virgin mother, lived among God's people, was hung on a cross until he died and on the third day conquered death and rose from the grave, we can be saved. No matter how sinful we are, we can be forgiven and not destroyed. God sent his Son so that we would not perish but could have eternal life. Why was it necessary for God to send his son and why was it necessary for Christ to die? The answer is that because, despite the beauty of the rainbow, it is only a sign. Signs won't do when what you need is a Savior. The rainbow is a reminder of kingdoms destroyed and a promise made, but the resurrected Christ gives us healing for today, as well as hope for tomorrow. No matter how close the arc of the rainbow seems or how much of the sky it covers, it cannot bridge the gap between humans and God; only Christ can do that. Our sins separate us from God, but Christ's cleansing blood washes our sins away. Through Christ, we are made acceptable to God. Christ was the sacrifice for man's sins. He became a sweet aroma to God. He was the spotless lamb sacrificed on the altar for your sins and mine. Psalm 34:8 say: "Taste and see that the LORD is good; blessed is the man who takes refuge in him." Without Christ, our "what next?" would have been hell and damnation, but because of Christ we can be saved.

No matter what your "what's next" has been in the past - a drink, a drug, whatever it might have been - you can be saved but only by Christ. So, commit yourself to maintaining an intimate relationship with God. Be patient and trust God. He will see you through. Be obedient and doors will be closed to protect you, and other doors will be opened to provide for you. If you are faithful to give thanks to God for your life and blessings, even the valleys, as well as the mountain top experiences, your sacrifices will be a sweet aroma to Him. You can be cleansed, washed of all unrighteousness. You can be saved by God's grace and receive his mercy. There is nothing that you have done, or can do, that can separate you from the love of God. If you'll confess your sins and accept Christ; if you will make Christ your Lord then you will not have to worry about "what's next?" because you will know that all of your "what's next" situations are directed by God.

Why don't you take this opportunity to establish your relationship with God? God has been patiently waiting for you. If you will put God first, make giving thanks to God your first priority, He will be pleased with your sacrifice. God will cover you during your storm, walk with you and speak to your heart. He will hear your prayers and your pleas.

God offers you reassuring rainbows after the storm. God offers you His Son.

The Invitation

Joshua began the closing of his sermon in a subdued voice. His family listened intently as he began to rehearse the invitation to accept Christ that he would deliver at the end of his sermon on Sunday. He opened the invitation by asking penetratingly personal questions. He hoped that the questions would resonate with people as they thought about their lives. He wanted each person to make an honest assessment of their circumstances and to determine for themselves if their relationship with God is what they wanted it to be. Success to Joshua as a preacher was not only educating people about God, but moving them to make a decision to accept Christ as their Lord and Saviour. Joshua's primary responsibility as a preacher, he believed, was to help people develop a close and effective personal relationship with Christ. "Are you at a place in your life where you are wondering what's next?" Joshua inquired. "Are you wrestling with questions of why you are here, what is your purpose in life, maybe even is life worth living? Have you tried to find answers to your questions but looked in all of the wrong places? Did you find out that bars did not hold the answer, nor did education, money, drugs, or unhealthy relationships? Are you sick and tired of trying to figure things out on your own? Are you tired of making poor choices, wrong turns and reaping a harvest of pain and sorrow? Today I ask you, are you willing to accept help from the only One who is able to guide you successfully through whatever comes next in your life? Will you turn now to the only One able to cradle you in an ark of safety? Who is that you ask? It is Jesus Christ. Christ is the answer to your questions. For you see, John 14:6 says that 'Jesus is the way, the truth and the light.' Christ will guide you through the darkness that is your life and will bring you safely through your storms. Will you accept His help today? Will you make Jesus the head of your life? Will you receive Him this moment? Will you make a decision right now that can change your life forever? Will you accept Christ today?"

"How, Pastor, you ask, do I receive Jesus Christ? The answer is not complicated; all you must do is believe that

Christ died for your sins and rose from the dead! Then pray, asking God to forgive your sins and Christ to come into your heart and your life. God will hear and answer a heartfelt, sincere and honest prayer as simple as this: 'Dear Jesus, I am sorry for the wrong things that I have done. Thank you for dying on the cross for my sins. Please forgive all my sins. Please come into my life and make me the kind of person you want me to be, forever! Amen!' "Accepting Jesus is a matter of believing and trusting in His promise that He will come into your life if you invite Him. He has already paid the price for your redemption. It is up to you to accept His gift. It does not depend on how you feel about it for it is already done. Nor do you have to understand everything the Bible says about Him; the Holy Spirit will teach you as you study and grow as a disciple. Know that Christ will never leave nor forsake you, not even in death! Thank Him! Amen!" Joshua's voice was loud and raspy at the close of his invitation, and then suddenly he was silent.

Joshua breathed an enormous sigh of relief. His family sat speechlessly for a moment, each person was absorbed in their own thoughts. Joshua stood watching them and searching each child's face for a sign that they had understood all that had been said. As their father and pastor he was eager for the day when they too would accept Christ as their Redeemer.

Jai was the first to break the silence. "Well, I guess I'll call Grandma and tell her that it is her turn to be part of Dad's sermon," Jai declared.

"Oh, she'll love it," Abigail chimed in.

"Better her than us, right?" Penny followed her siblings in their joking.

"You know it," Abigail agreed.

"Dad, you never disappoint us on Freak Out Friday," Jai continued his teasing.

Joshua did not respond. He simply smiled at his wife and kids. He took their teasing in stride. Joshua was satisfied that the light hearted banter of his kids meant that they had no idea about the tragedies in the lives of the people that inspired the sermon. "My member's confessions will always be their pastor's secrets." Joshua thought to himself. Then he inhaled deeply, closed his manuscript and said, "Okay, let's get to the pet store before it closes. I understand thirty-seven guppies and their mom need a new home."

Chapter 6: Zarina's Decision

Branford had looked forward to his Monday meeting with Zarina since Friday, when Junior Leigh let it slip that she had made an appointment with Clarissa his secretary to see him. He was anxious to know what she had decided about revealing the fact that she was HIV positive to her unsuspecting prom date.

"Hi Zarina," Clarissa said to the teenage girl walking into her office who was looking down in the dumps.

"Hello," Zarina's response was barely audible.

"Like your new hairstyle," Clarissa remarked hoping to cheer her up a little.

"Thanks, I wanted to try out a few new styles before the big night," Zarina said referring to her upcoming prom.

"It looks great. Are you excited?" Clarissa continued.

"Yes, a little," Zarina said.

"I am sure that everything is going to be just lovely. The Pastor is expecting you so you can go right in. Or would you rather wait for Junior to get here before you go in; referring to Samuel Leigh, Jr., Zarina's prom date?"

"No, I'll go right in. I want to tell the pastor something before Junior gets here, if that is okay."

"Sure," Clarissa said. "I will just buzz his office to let him know that you are here."

"Okay, thank you."

"Pastor, Zarina is here," Clarissa said into the phone.

"Okay, send her in," the pastor's voice boomed back over the intercom.

Zarina walked down the short hallway to the Pastor's office absorbed in thoughts of what she was about to do.

"Well, hello movie star," the Pastor teased Zarina as she came into his office.

"Pastor," Zarina said shyly and took a seat in front of the pastor's desk.

"So, what brings you in today?" Branford asked, believing that he already knew the answer.

"Well, I thought about what you said, and I even read the story of Queen Esther that you told me about. So, I've decided that I will tell Junior that I am HIV positive. That is, as long as you make him promise before I tell him that nothing that is said in this office can be repeated outside of the office. Can you do that?" Zarina asked.

"Sure, I can ask him to promise not to say anything to anyone else. But you know that I can't make him keep that promise, right." Branford wanted to make sure that Zarina was well informed and aware of the possible consequences of her decision.

"Yes, I know that. I have thought about it a lot and I know that Junior is a good person. I don't think that he would break his promise especially to you. If I did, I would not tell him."

"Okay. So how do you want to handle this?" the pastor asked.

"When Junior comes in to meet with us, you ask him. I will go out of the room, so he won't feel pressured to agree. If he says yes, I will tell him. If he says no, I won't and that will be that."

"Okay. And if he says yes you have decided to tell him despite the fact that he might not want to be your friend after this, or to take you to the prom as his date. Is that right?"

"Yes, to be perfectly honest I am tired of pretending that I am not sick. I am tired of hiding from people and always waiting for something bad to happen. Like Queen Esther, I am ready to say, I am who I am and that is that."

"And if he says that he can't promise to keep everything a secret, what then?" Branford asked

"I will tell him that I can't be his friend anymore. Maybe, I will tell him that my grandmother thinks that I am too young to go to the prom, which she does, anyway."

"All right then, I will leave that up to you," Branford said.

Zarina clasped her hands together as if praying and said, "Pastor, I want to tell Junior now, but I am not ready to tell the world, yet. I am still working on that. I want to see how this works out first."

"I understand, and I think that this is a step in the right direction. I am proud of you Zarina."

"Thanks," the pretty little girl said.

"So, exactly how do you expect things to go today?" the pastor asked.

"What do you mean?"

"Do you expect Junior to say that it is okay, it does not matter? Or are you expecting him to be angry or upset? What exactly do you think is going to happen?"

"Well, I think that he will be surprised and I hope that he won't be angry or anything. I'm not sure what to expect. I never had to do anything like this before. I am not sure how he will react but I am willing to take a chance and see what will happen. I know that if it goes badly that he is only one person in this world. There are many others that I will tell who will not react the same way. I also know that there will be some people that will have negative reactions. But no matter how he reacts, I am just ready to get it over with now."

"What does your grandmother think? She must be relieved that you are going to tell him."

"No, not yet. I did not tell her that I am going to tell him. You and I are going to call her when this meeting is over and tell her together. I don't think that she would believe me if I told her alone anyway."

"Okay. Although, I think that you should give your grandmother more credit than that. I think that she would believe you if you said that you told Junior, but I am willing to tell her with you."

"Then I guess we are all set. Now, all we need is for Junior to show up for the meeting," the pastor said

"Oh, I am sure that he will," Zarina said. "He promised that he would."

As if on cue, Clarissa buzzed in to say that Junior was in the outer office and to ask if it was okay to send him in.

"Yes, please send him in," the pastor responded.

"Hi," Junior said as he came through the office door. He smiled at Zarina and said, "Sorry I'm a little late."

"It's okay; it gave me a chance to talk to the pastor for a minute."

"Will you excuse me, please? I will be right back." Zarina said as she stood to leave the room.

"Sure," the pastor said.

"Sure," Junior said a little surprised by Zarina's quick exist.

"Well, Junior," the pastor said, trying to think of an ice breaker. "How was dinner, after your parents renewed their vows?"

"It was great. They are very happy and so am I."

"Good."

"I am glad that everything worked out so well for the three of you."

"Yeah, me too."

"I know that you must be curious about why Zarina asked you to come to meet with us today," Branford said.

"Sure, I thought that it had something to do with some project or something that she wants to do. That is it right?" Junior asked the question slowly. Still not sure why Zarina had left so abruptly.

"In a sense yes, but not exactly," the pastor said.

"Then what is it," Junior asked.

"Well, before we get into that, I have to ask you to promise to do something and I need you to really think about this before you make a decision," the pastor cautioned.

"That sounds serious," the surprised Junior said.

"I need you to make a promise to me and to Zarina that anything revealed to you in this room will not be repeated outside of this office to anyone under any circumstances."

"You guys can't possibly be planning anything illegal right?" Junior asked with a hint of humor in his voice.

"No, of course not, no it is not anything like that," Branford said.

"Did anything happen to Zarina?" Junior asked more seriously.

"No, it is just my policy that when people are in a counseling session with me that all parties agree that nothing said during the session is repeated by any of the parties attending the session. You can understand that right?"

"Yeah, but is this a counseling session. I thought we were meeting because Zarina wanted to talk about a project."

"Yes, if we go forward it will be a counseling session," the pastor made Junior aware of the situation.

"Oh," Junior said an expression of confusion was on his face.

"How old are you Junior?"

"Eighteen," he answered.

"Okay, that's good," the pastor said before continuing. "I am going to give you this form to read and sign. Please sign it only if you agree to keep everything confidential. After you have made your decision, I will ask Zarina to come in and we can get started. Is that okay with you?"

"Sure, but I have not done anything to Zarina. I promise you that, Pastor," Junior said, now seeming more worried than confused.

"I know son, this is not about anything that you have done. Don't worry about that. It is just that we might say some things that none of us would want repeated outside of this room. Okay."

Branford opened his desk and pulled out a confidentiality form and handed it to Junior. Junior read the short form over, signed it and gave it back to the pastor.

"Thank you. Did you understand everything?" Branford asked.

"Yes. Will Zarina sign the same form?" Junior probed.

"Yes, she will," Branford assured him.

Branford picked up the phone dialed his secretary's extension and said, "Clarissa will you ask Zarina to come back in, please."

Shortly afterwards, the door crept opened and Zarina stepped timidly back into the office.

The pastor waved his hand at Zarina beckoning her to the empty seat in front of his desk next to Junior. Zarina sat down and waited to learn the outcome of the conversation between the pastor and Junior.

"Zarina," the pastor began, "Will you promise to keep all of the conversations that take place in this office between the three of us confidential."

"Yes, if the two of you will promise to keep everything confidential as well."

"That is fair enough. Junior has already signed a confidentiality agreement. Here is one for you to sign and I will sign one as well. Agreed?"

"Sure," Zarina said as she reached for the form the pastor was handing to her.

Zarina glanced at the familiar form, quickly signed it with the pastor's silver pen that had been standing in its matching holder on the desk. When she finished, she gave the form back him. Branford signed his form and put the three signed documents back into his desk draw.

"Now, we can get down to the reason for this meeting," Branford said.

Junior had a look like a deer caught in headlights on his face as he waited for the pastor to inform him of the reason for their meeting. He was even more confused when Zarina started talking instead of the pastor, as he had expected.

"Junior, first I want to say thank you for being my friend. I like spending time with you and I hope that you feel the same way about me."

Junior was beginning to feel as if he were being put on the spot but said, "I like you too, Zarina. What exactly is this about?" Junior wanted to dispense with the small talk. He was ready to learn the reason for the meeting.

"I want to tell you something," Zarina continued. "Something that is hard for me to say. So I am only going to say it once, okay. You don't have to say anything after I say it. I don't want you to feel as if you have to say anything or do anything. I just want you to know because I want to be honest with you, okay."

"Okay, just spit it out. Whatever it is I am sure that I will be okay with it. Just tell me."

"Okay. I am HIV positive," Zarina said into her hands which she had put up in front of her face.

"You are what!" Junior exclaimed.

Zarina did not answer.

Branford who had been silent during the exchange between Zarina and Junior spoke up.

"Yes, Junior, you heard correctly. Zarina is HIV positive. She wanted you to know that because you are her friend."

"When did this happen? How," Junior asked excitedly.

"I was infected about two years ago," Zarina answered removing her hands from in front of her face.

"And you are just telling me now! Why didn't you tell me before?" the animated boy asked twisting in his seat to look directly at Zarina.

"I was afraid that if I told you, you would not want to be my friend."

"Why?"

"I don't know. That is just how people are," Zarina said shrugging her shoulders.

"You think that I am like other people?" Junior seethed, and said with clinched teeth. "Don't you know that my Dad just got out of jail for shooting my uncle? Do you realize how many parents won't let their kids be around me because they think I might be a bad influence, not because of anything that I have done, but because of who my father is?"

Junior's tirade continued, "Do you know how many friends I've lost over the past few years? Didn't you understand any of what I told you about me and my

273

family? I can't believe this, I thought that you were my friend, but you never trusted me at all, did you?

"I do trust you. That is why I am telling you now. That is what this is all about," Zarina said as tears began to roll down her cheeks.

"How did this happen to you?" Junior quieted himself a little in response to his friend's tears. "I thought you said that you are a virgin. Did you get a blood transfusion or something?"

"No, I did not get it through a transfusion," Zarina admitted to Junior.

"What happened then? How did you get infected?"

"It doesn't matter. I just am, it just happened, okay."

"No, it didn't just happen and I want to know what happened. I want to know if you have been lying to me all of this time," Junior said incensed.

"I am, sort of a virgin, I," Zarina started to explain.

Junior interrupted Zarina tersely and said, "There is no such thing as sort of a virgin. You either are or you are not. Is that how you got infected?"

"No. Please Junior, don't make me say what happened. It is too embarrassing."

"To embarrassing. Jezzz, Zarina, I told you so many things about my family, things that I never shared with anyone. Things that I would be embarrassed if anyone ever found out and I never once asked you to sign a paper saying that you would keep everything a secret. I trusted you because I thought that you were my friend. Why couldn't you tell me? Why didn't you do the same thing with me?"

"I was afraid. I'm sorry, Junior. You always treated me with so much respect. Like I was a real Christian. You know how you always calling me a virgin princess. You were the last person that I wanted to know that I was with some guy that I didn't really even know, that I did something so stupid.

"He was your boyfriend," Junior asked.

"No, he was just some guy I met at a friend's house. We ditched school and did some stupid things. We did things that were supposed to be fun. I know now that that they were just stupid. I was with him just once and I got infected."

"That's rough," Junior said.

"Yes, it is. I just wanted to pretend that none of it happened. Start over. That is what really happened okay. Now you know."

Junior leaned back in his chair for a moment processing Zarina's words. He took a deep breath and then said, "I understand. I've been there. Everybody makes mistakes, sometimes big ones. I know that very well considering what my family has been through, but I still don't get it. You don't look sick."

"I know, neither did the guy I got infected by, and actually I am in pretty good health for someone with the virus. Lots of people who are infected don't look sick. I learned that the hard way."

Then Zarina said again, "I'm sorry, Junior. I thought that if you knew you might not want to be my friend. I thought you might decide that you didn't want to hang around with me, or take me to the prom or anything like that. I was being selfish I guess. I didn't want you to treat me differently. I wanted to fit in, to feel normal and you seemed so normal. You had the life I wanted. You are on the track team. You have friends and you do normal stuff."

"Zarina, don't you realize that they call it a track team but almost everybody on the track is doing individual stuff. You run for the school team yeah, but you run by yourself," Junior said shaking his head. "And what is normal, Zarina? Having a father in jail, family members on drugs, little cousins being abused, mother worried about your father having HIV? What the heck is normal, Zarina? What in the world did you see in my life that was normal?" Junior badgered Zarina with rage again in his voice.

Zarina professed, "I never thought about it that way, Junior. I only thought about me, and how being friends

277

with you made me feel. I thought about what would happen to me if you found out. So, I never told you, but now that I did what will happen to us?"

"I don't know. I will have to think about that. I just don't know and not because you are HIV positive but because you did not trust me enough to tell me. And because I feel like you lied to me by keeping it a secret."

"But I am telling you now. That should count for something," Zarina's eyes filled once again with tears.

"I hear you, but you knew that for weeks I had been worried about my Dad coming home. I told you that my Mom was concerned about him being HIV positive. I even told you that they were going to get tested. I told you everything and you told me nothing."

"Please Junior. I'm sorry, I just never thought about any of that. Even though you told me all about what was going on with you, I still thought that I was different. Since this happened to me I've felt like I was alone, that I was the only one going through a problem like this one. You worrying about whether or not your Dad might have the disease did not seem the same to me, as me actually having the disease," Zarina said emphasizing the word actually. You were saying that your Dad could be positive or he could not be positive. I am positive; there is no doubt about that. I didn't think that your knowing about me would help you."

"Didn't you understand how worried I was about my Dad? I worried about how I would react if he was infected. I worried about what life would be like for him if he was. I was nervous about what it would mean to my parents' relationship, I even worried that he would be sick and possibly dying. You could have said at any time, look at me. I'm infected and I'm okay. That would have meant the world to me, Zarina."

"I'm so sorry. I didn't realize that Junior, please forgive me." Zarina said to Junior with passion in her voice.

The she turned to the pastor and said something that he was pleased to hear. "That is what you tried to help me see, Pastor, that I could actually help people by sharing my story, but I did not get it until now."

The pastor nodded, acknowledging Zarina's observation, thinking that she was changing from a selfish adolescent princess into a compassionate young queen before his eyes. "My Queen Esther," the pastor thought.

Once again the pastor broke into the conversation between Zarina and the upset young man sitting in front of him, "Junior, when you thought that your father might be infected, did you ever think of how the world, your family, friends, and neighbors might react to him or to you if they found out."

"Sure, that was one of the main reasons I was so worried," Junior confessed to the Branford.

"If you understand how people can react, then can you just for a moment, possibly begin to think about what it was like for Zarina trying to decide if she should tell you?"

"I guess," Junior said begrudgingly.

"You know that people can be cruel, don't you, son? Some people have been cruel to you because of your father, right?"

"Yes, very mean at times," Junior admitted.

"And some people will make Zarina's life very hard if they find out about her disease. You understand that."

"Yes."

"Then please don't be too hard on her for trying to protect herself from hurtful and painful situations by keeping her condition quiet," Branford interceded on Zarina's behalf.

"I get that, I'm just angry because she did not have enough faith in me to tell me. I am just disappointed that while I was telling her all about my life, she was holding back things about hers."

"I understand that, and I think that she does too," Branford acknowledged.

"Yes, I do," Zarina was quick to respond to the pastor's statement.

"So, what now?" Junior asked.

"What would the two of you like to happen?" the pastor asked of both Junior and Zarina.

Zarina was the first to speak up. "Junior," she said, "I hope that you will forgive me, and I hope that we can still be friends."

Junior looked at Zarina, and then asked snidely, "Is there anything else that you want to tell me?"

"No," she said. "Nothing else."

"Are you sure?"

"Yes," she reassured him.

"Then I guess we are still friends, nothing that you have said has changed that. If you can put up with the craziness of my life then I can put up with the craziness of yours."

"Thank you," Zarina said and burst into sobs.

"For what? What now?"

"For being my friend silly," she said through the tears.

"No, you just don't realize that for a minute, when the pastor started talking about keeping everything a secret. I thought that the two of you were going to tell me that you were in love or something. Then I thought oh, no, that can't be, maybe she is going to tell me that she is really a boy. I mean I was actually sitting here thinking to myself, "Please, say it ain't so. Just say it ain't so!"

Junior stopped talking for a second then said, "Zarina, you are not, are you? I mean a boy or anything," he asked with a quirky look on his face.

"No, I am definitely not a boy!" Zarina yelled.

The trio simultaneously burst into laughter.

"And the prom is still on," Branford asked knowing that it was important to Zarina to be certain about that.

"Yes, as far as I am concerned it is," Junior said.

"Me too," Zarina confirmed excitedly.

"That's great," Branford was glad to have them both agree to go to the prom together, especially since Zarina had taken so much delight in planning for it.

"Pastor," Zarina said suddenly. "Can we call my grandmother now and tell her that Junior knows about my condition?"

"I don't see why not," he answered.

"Junior will you stay while we call my grandmother. I want the pastor to put her on speaker phone and tell her that I've told you that I am HIV positive. You can tell her too, that you know and that you understand what that means. Is that okay."

"Sure, but I thought that we promised not to tell anyone outside of the office what was said in the office." Junior reminded them.

"You are right," Branford said. "Zarina's grandmother already knows about her condition, that was what we were worried about keep secret, and she was very concerned about you not knowing, too".

Zarina chimed in, "Yes, she thought that something might happen between us and that you would get sick."

"Oh, I see. Didn't you tell her that we are just friends?"

"Yes, but she did not believe me. She has it in her head that we are or could be more than that."

"So, can we all agree that we can call Zarina's grandmother and tell her that you know?"

"Yes, let's do that, please, okay Junior?" Zarina asked.

"Sure." Junior said, "Zarina I read up a lot on HIV and Aids because of my Dad, but is there anything special that I should know. You know, in case anything ever happens and you need help."

"No, just don't wig out on me and everything will be fine. We can talk about all of that stuff later, okay?"

"Sure."

"Can I ask you something, Junior?" Zarina's tone became more serious.

"Sure. What?"

"If I did decide to tell people that I am HIV positive will you still be my friend. If people know about me and they know that we are friends, they might think that you are sick too; or other weird things. They might be rotten to you."

"Zarina, I will be your friend no matter what you decide to do. You can tell people or not tell people that is up to you. Just let me know what it is that you are going through. I'm your friend. I've got your back."

"Thank you."

"Well, I am proud of both of you," Branford chimed in.

"Thank you." they both said.

"Before we call Zarina's grandmother let's pray, okay," the pastor requested.

"Sure," the two agreed. Both Junior and Zarina bowed their heads as Rev. Branford launched into his prayer.

"Lord, we all thank you that today some things just ain't so," Branford said, referring to Junior's comment that he thought that reason for the confidentiality form might be because the pastor, and Zarina, were going to reveal to him that they were in love. Or that they were going to inform him that Zarina was really a boy. When Zarina and Junior heard the pastor's prayer their bowed heads popped up in astonishment and their closed eyes flew open wide with surprise. They all laughed out loud and, Junior cried, "Halleluiah, Amen!"

Thank you for purchasing
♥The Pastor's Secrets♥

Volume 2 of the
Pastor's Secrets
will be available
July 2013
With a special sermon by
Minister William H.
Simmons, III

Order your copy on
Amazon.com

Follow us on Twitter

@pastorssecrets

Like us on Facebook at

http://www.facebook.com/Th

ePastorsSecrets

Visit our webpage

tpsbydbs.com

www.ingramcontent.com/pod-product-compliance
Lightning Source LLC
Chambersburg PA
CBHW051816090426
42736CB00011B/1507